MASTERING CHORDS AND CHORD PROGRESSIONS FOR THE UKULELE

VOL. 2

> Build on your basic chord knowledge to create movable chord shapes, jazzy extensions, and simple chord melodies!

BRAD BENEFIELD

Mastering Chords and Chord Progressions for the Ukulele, Vol. 2

"Build on your basic chord knowledge to create movable chord shapes, jazzy extensions, and moving chord melodies."

Author: Brad Benefield

Copyright © 2020 by Spotted Belly Books, Seattle, WA
www.SpottedBellyBooks.com

Printed by CreateSpace, An Amazon.com Company
May, 2020

All rights reserved. No part of this publication may be reproduced, distributed, or transmitted in any form or by any means, including photocopying, recording, or other electronic or mechanical methods, without the prior written permission of the publisher, except in the case of brief quotations embodied in critical reviews and certain other noncommercial uses permitted by copyright law.

TABLE OF CONTENTS

INTRODUCTION 1

CHAPTER 1 - MOVABLE CHORD FORMS 3

CHAPTER 2 - 7TH EXTENSIONS 26

CHAPTER 3 - THE JAZZIER SIDE 34

CHAPTER 4 - CHORD MELODIES 64

CHAPTER 5 - MOVING LINES 73

CHAPTER 6 - SUSPENDED CHORDS 76

CHAPTER 7 - OK, JUST A LITTLE MORE JAZZ 78

INTRODUCTION

This book continues where "Mastering Chords and Chord Progressions for Ukulele Vol. 1" left off, and the philosophy remains the same - at the heart of the ukulele is the ability to accompany the human voice with simple, but beautiful, chords. This book will take your chord playing to the next level, helping you navigate the neck of the ukulele, enhancing your basic chords with new sounds, tackling more complex jazz chords, and filling out your sound by adding simple melodies to your chords.

ABOUT THIS BOOK

This book continues our journey to master what you do on the ukulele 98% of the time - play basic chords to accompany yourself or another singer. The exercises in this book concentrate on:

- Learning the basic movable forms for the major, minor, and dominant 7th chords up and down the neck.
- Connecting these chords in progressions to minimize left-hand shifting.
- Learning the extensions for major 7th and minor 7th chords and applying them to jazzy vamps and progressions.

WHAT YOU SHOULD KNOW

To get the most from this book, you should have worked through most or all of Volume One of this series. Seriously, I'm not just trying to sell more books – the concepts, exercises and tips in Volume One are the foundation for the concepts presented in this book. There is a brief review of Volume One in this book but working through all the chords and progression in Volume One will really solidify the techniques used in Volume Two.

PRACTICE TIPS

- **Tune up** – I'm always amazed at how often I hear people playing out-of-tune ukuleles. Invest in a tuner, or tuner app, and just make it a habit to tune up whenever you pick up your ukulele.
- **Go slowly, but not quietly** - When you are learning anything new on the ukulele, it's much more efficient to take it slow at first. It's all about muscle memory, and our muscles learn best through slow repetition. However, don't mistake _slow_ for _quiet_. Even when you're practicing something slowly, be conscious of getting a solid sound and tone.
- **Take small bites** - If there's a chord or a section of a song that is giving you trouble, stop and isolate it, and practice just that part. Sometimes that means repeating two chords over and over, sometimes it's a particular strumming pattern, but if you just keep blowing past it, it will always be a weak spot in your playing.
- **Let people hear you** – "But, I sound horrible!" No, you don't. YOU ALWAYS SOUND BETTER THAN YOU THINK YOU DO. Don't worry about other people - just play, make music, and enjoy it!

READING THE EXERCISES

Most of the exercises consist of chord diagrams, or grids, over a music staff with a basic rhythm indicated. For this book, I haven't included any strumming variations like there were in Volume One. However, you can easily apply those variations to the exercises in this book.

ENHARMONICS

"Enharmonic" is a fancy way of saying, "two chords, or notes, that sound the same, but have different names". Without going into details about the music theory behind it, just be aware that some chords will have two different names, but be fingered exactly the same, depending on what the key is. In some of the examples in this book, you will see that:

- Ab is the same as G#
- Db is the same as C#
- Eb is the same as D#
- Gb is the same as F#

CHAPTER 1 - MOVABLE CHORD FORMS

REVIEWING THE BASICS

Let's start off with a quick review of the 36 basic chord forms from Volume One: 12 major chords, 12 minor chords, and 12 dominant 7th chords.

The 12 major chords in open position

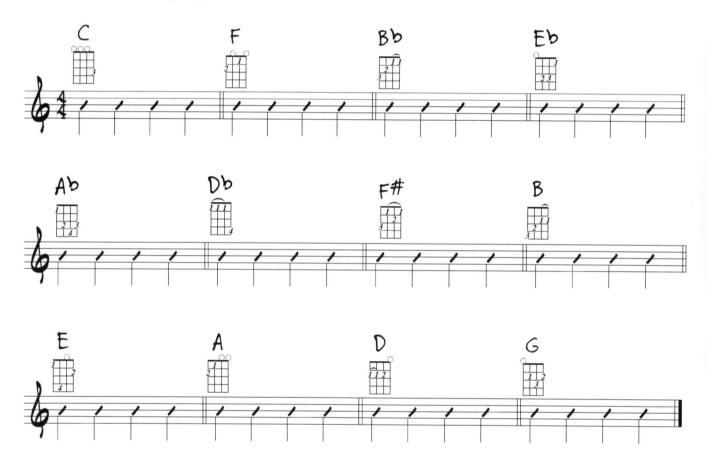

The 12 minor chords in open position

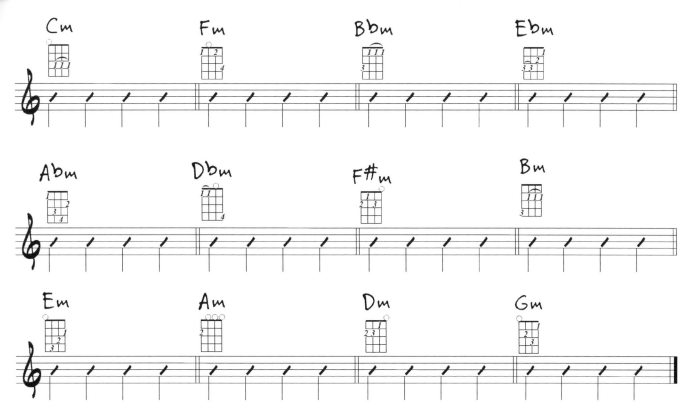

The 12 dominant 7th chords in open position

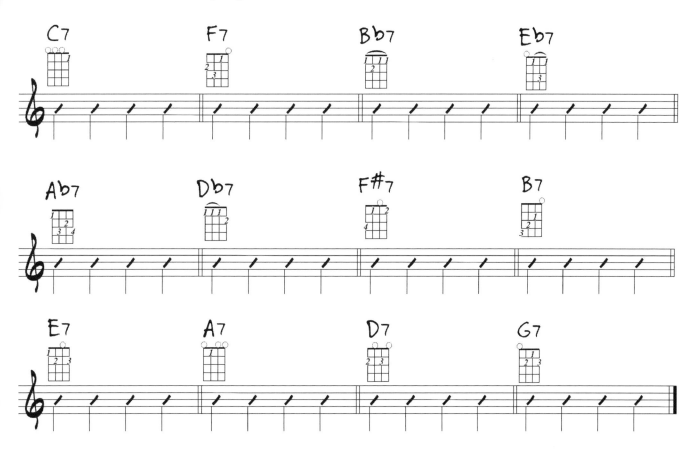

MOVABLE CHORD FORMS

So, one of the goals of Volume One was to simplify things so you only needed to remember one single chord form for any particular chord. Now, we're going to complicate things a little by adding alternate forms for each chord.

In Volume One, we dealt mostly with open position chords – that is, all of the chords (whenever possible) contained at least one open string. In this section, you'll learn the basic closed, or **movable** chord forms. They're called **movable** forms because they don't use open strings, and because of this they can be moved up and down the neck. For example, if you know a movable form for D, you can simply move it up two frets and get an E chord. Or three frets for an F chord, and five frets for a G chord.

NOTE: Given that the ukulele has a pretty short neck, in this book we generally won't go past the 7th fret. While you are welcome to experiment with playing as far up the neck as you like, the sound quality starts to deteriorate on most ukuleles and it gets very "plinky".

The following exercises introduces your fingers to the closed forms by taking the open forms you already know and moving them up the neck chromatically. Run through these exercises many times to get your fingers used to the forms. Even after you've learned the forms, this still makes a good warm-up exercise.

Ex. 1 Movable major chords

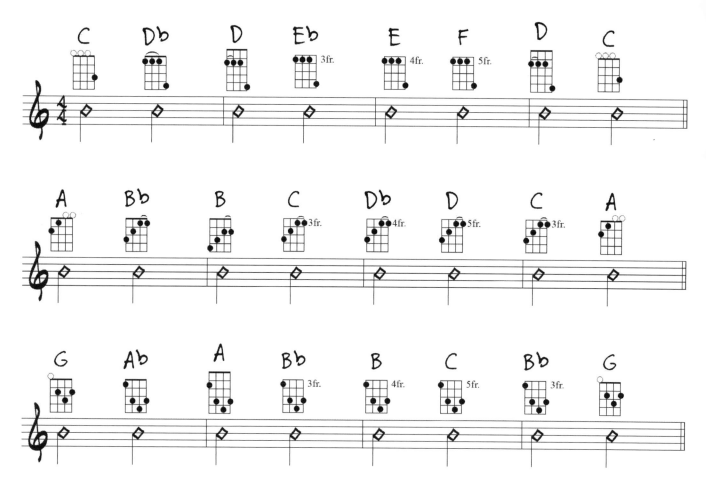

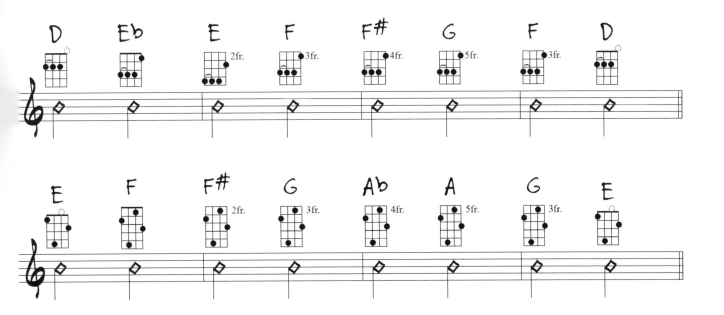

Ex.2 Movable minor chords

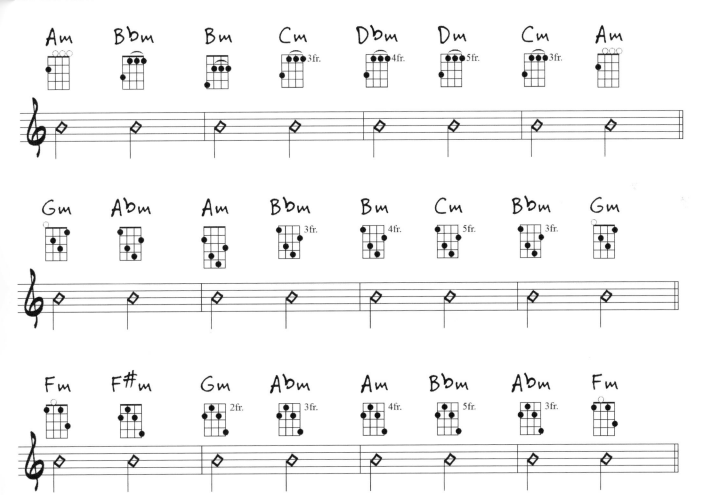

Ex. 3 Movable dominant 7th chords

CONNECTING OPEN CHORDS AND MOVABLE CHORDS

So, that's all the chords you need right there. But it's not very convenient, even as a general reference. In order to be able to use these alternate forms in your everyday playing, you need to make the connections between the forms for each chord. The next three exercises help you do just that. Spend some time on these - the more comfortable you are with these exercises, the easier the rest of the concepts in the book will be.

Ex. 4 *Connecting open and closed major chords*

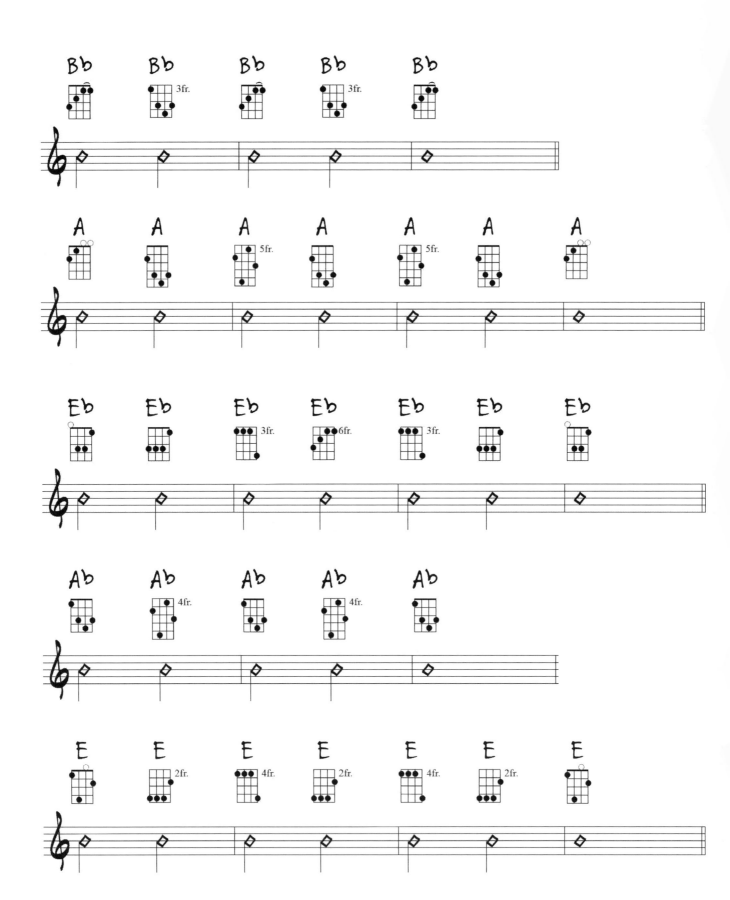

Ex. 5 Connecting open and closed minor chords

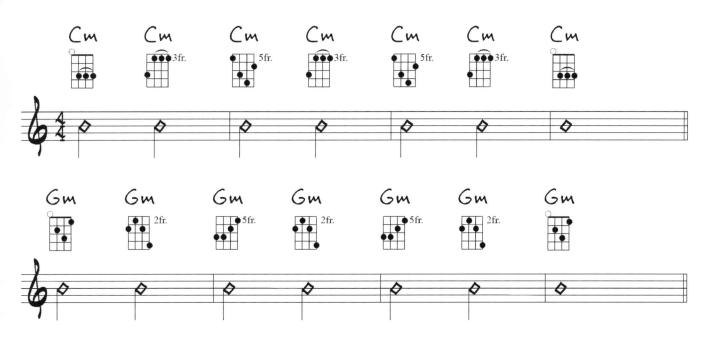

Ex. 6 Connecting open and closed dominant 7th chords

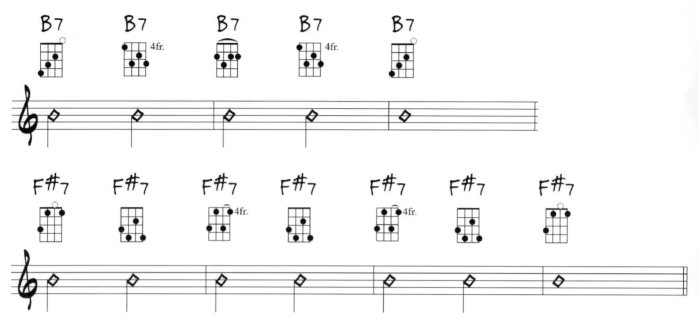

NOTE: Play these exercises a lot to get the muscle memory into your fingers so you don't have to think too much, for example, about where another F chord might be – your fingers will just know. **This won't happen overnight,** but if you practice these exercises regularly, it will happen sooner than you think.

COMBINING CHORDS IN PROGRESSIONS

Now that you're getting more comfortable moving around the neck, let's make those movements more efficient by learning some common connections between chords. The following exercises work on connecting I – V chords and I – IV chords (and their minor equivalents) in ways with as little shifting as necessary.

NOTE: As mentioned in the last exercise, practice these connections a lot so your fingers start to make the connections automatically.

Ex. 7 Connecting chords in a I - V progression

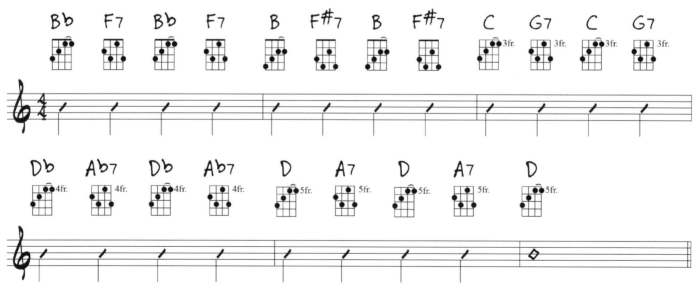

- 15 -

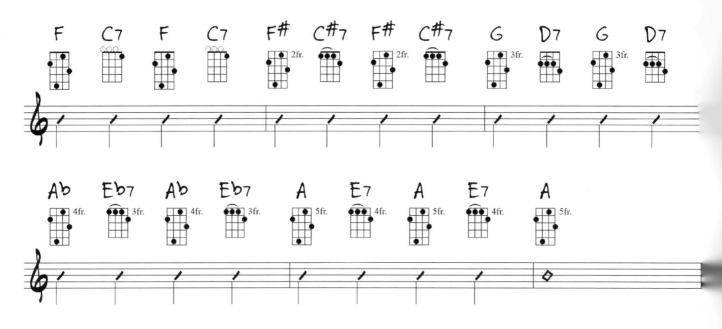

Ex. 8 Connecting chords in a I - IV progression

Ex. 9 *Connecting minor chords in a i - V progression*

Ex. 10 Connecting minor chords in a i - iv progression

Let's take those connections and apply them to a full progression now. The exercises on the next pages have a variety of connections for a popular I – vi – IV – V7 progression in the keys of C, G, D, A, and E.

Ex. 11 Open and closed chords in a I - vi - ii V progression

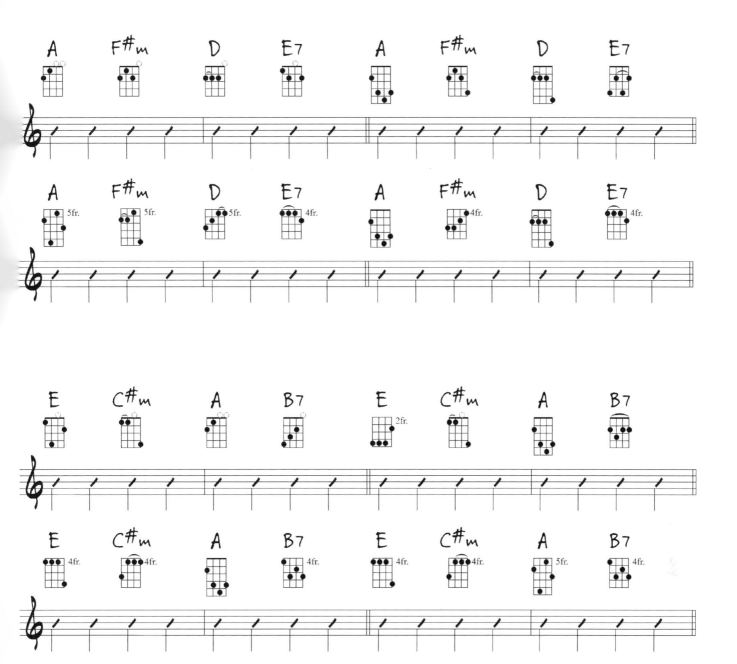

And that's it for the basics of movable chords. By practicing the above exercises, you will:

- Know at least three, and sometimes four, different versions of each chord in every key.
- Know how to move a single chord to different positions to add some variety to your playing.
- Know how to connect common chords efficiently.

To really get these under your fingers, I strongly suggest going back to the different chord progressions in Volume One and practice mixing in open chords and closed chords, as we did with the last exercise. There are hundreds of possible combinations you can create – I can't write them all down, and you can't possibly learn all of them, but don't let that overwhelm you. Just by applying a few different chord forms to each progression, you will discover ones that you like to play and sound good to you. You may also discover that you prefer different chord forms for different keys. When you feel more comfortable with some of the movable forms, apply them to songs that you already know and play to add some variety.

For a quick refresher, here are the progressions that we covered in Volume One:

I – V – I	I – vi – IV – V – I	I – IV – iv – I
I – IV – I	I – ii – IV – I	I – III7 – IV – I
I – IV – V – I	I – ii – iii – ii – I	i – iv – bVI7 – V7 – I
I – V – IV – I	I – V – vi – IV – I	i – bVII – bVI – V7
IV – V – I	i – iv – V – i	I – bVII – IV – I
V – IV – I	I – VI7 – II7 – V7 – I	I – bIII – IV – I
IV – I – V – I	I – II7 – IV – I	I – bII – bIII – bII – I

CHAPTER 2 - 7TH EXTENSIONS

OVERVIEW OF 7TH CHORDS

In this chapter, we'll move into the world of 7th chords. You already know the dominant 7th chord, which has been our "V" (five) chord, as in C – F – G7 – C, but we never really talked about what a 7th chord is. We only mentioned that it has an extra note in the chord. There are two other 7th chords to learn – the **major 7** (written maj7) and the **minor 7** (written min7).

NOTE: There is much more to the music theory of building chords. A basic search on Google will give you tons of resources to browse. You don't need to know the following information to play any of the exercises in this book, but it's provided just in case you want to investigate it further.

You'll remember that every scale has corresponding numbers to identify the degrees of the scale, for example:

Key of C:	C	D	E	F	G	A	B
Scale degree:	1	2	3	4	5	6	7

So, we know that a I – IV – V progression in C is C - F - G7. Well, the same numbers apply to building a chord from a scale. For any scale, the I chord will be built from the I, 3, and 5 of the scale. In the case of C, a C chord contains the notes C, E, and G.

This "every other note" pattern can also build other chords. For example, still using our C scale example, the ii chord, or Dm, is D, F, and A – starting on D and selecting every other note. The F chord, or the IV chord, would be F, A, C, and the G chord would be G, B, D.

But what about G7? We simply continue to skip every other note and get G, B, D, F to make the G7 chord - the F is the 7th.

This same idea can be applied to create our next two 7th chords – the major 7th and the minor 7th. By simply skipping every other note, we can build a C major 7 chord (Cmaj7) with C, E, G, B and a D minor 7 chord (Dm7) with D, F, A, C.

The maj7 and min7 chords aren't really new chords to learn – they're an "enhanced substitute" for any major or minor chord (except a V chord). For example, the progression C – Am – F – G could also be played as Cmaj7 – Am7 – Fmaj7 – G7. Functionally, it is the same progression. However, whether to substitute the 7th chords is completely up to you and how you like, or dislike, the sound in that particular situation.

NOTE: I want to emphasize this again – in most cases, any major chord can be a maj7, and any minor chord can be a min7. It all depends on what YOU think sounds good. Pay attention to what the different types sound like and what you like to play and what you don't – this is your own style that you are developing.

OPEN POSITION 7TH CHORDS

Let's get started and see how to turn our open string chords into 7th chords. We'll start with the maj7 chords.

Ex. 12   Open position maj7 chords, all keys

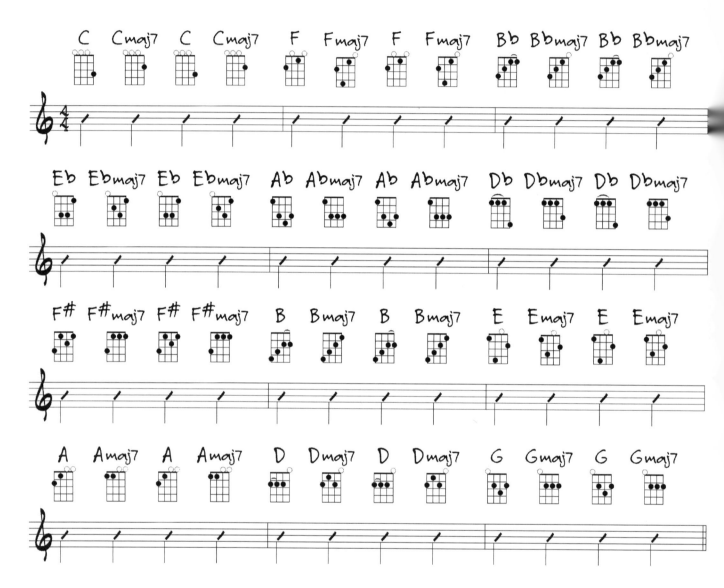

Now go back to Volume One and play through some of the progressions substituting maj7 chords for the major chords. You'll probably notice that some keys sound better to you than others, and that's fine. Let your ears be your guide as to which sounds suit your personal style.

Next, let's add the min7 chords.

13 Open position min7 chords, all keys

Go back to Volume One and play through some progressions again, substituting min7 chords for any minor chords. Just substitute the minor chords at first, then substitute both the minors and the majors.

CLOSED POSITION 7TH CHORDS

Here are the closed position forms for the maj7 and min7 chords.

Ex. 14   Closed position maj7 chords, all keys

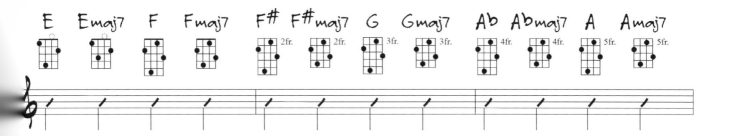

x. 15 **Closed position min7 chords, all keys**

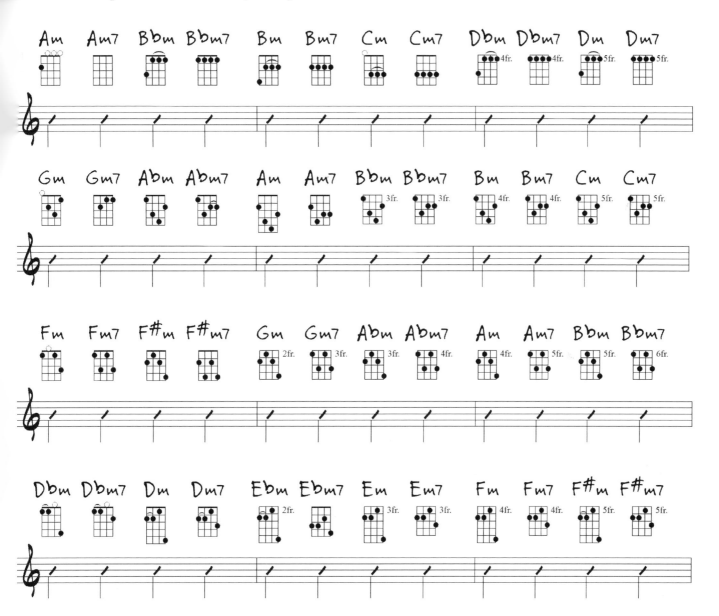

Again, go back to Volume One and play through some progressions, substituting major 7th and minor 7ths, in both open and closed forms. Here are a few examples of adding major 7th and minor 7th chords to a I vi IV V progression.

Ex. 16 *Closed position I - vi - IV - V progression*

SPEND SOME TIME ON THIS CHAPTER BEFORE MOVING ON. Learning the maj7 and min7 forms and integrating them naturally into your playing is the foundation of just about everything you'll do.

> Everything else that follows in this book is kind of icing on the cake – they are fun things you can do with chords, but you **HAVE TO KNOW AND HEAR THE CHORDS FIRST**.

As I mentioned before, there are an almost unlimited number of combinations that you can come up with for playing even a basic I – V – I progression. Just experiment with a few combinations for a progression and then move to another progression or move to another key. Doing a little bit every day will slowly but surely build your chord skills.

THE DIMINISHED 7TH CHORD

The diminished 7th chord is one of the most uniquely identifiable chords in music. The "diminished" name refers to the 5th and the 7th of the chord. You can also think of it as a min7 chord with the 5th and the 7th lowered an additional half-step. The following table shows how notes are lowered to progress from a major 7th chord to a dominant 7th to a minor 7th to a diminished 7th. The diminished 7th chord is written with the **"o7"** symbol.

Cmaj7		C7		Cmin7		Co7
C		C		C		C
E		E	>>>	Eb		Eb
G		G		G	>>>	Gb
B	>>>	Bb		Bb	>>>	A

The diminished chord has one interesting feature - it's a "symmetrical" chord. That is, the notes that make up the chords are all the same distance apart. Because all the notes are equidistant from each other, that means the chord repeats itself every three frets: Bo7 = Do7 = Fo7 = Abo7. This is a very typical sound of the diminished chord:

Ex. 17   Repeating diminished chord

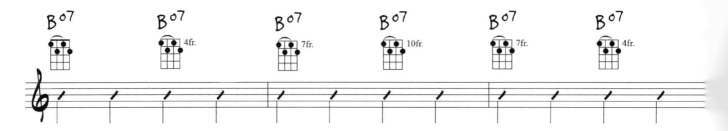

For our purposes, the diminished chord is used as substitute for the dom7 chord. Each diminished 7th chord contains three notes from a related dom7 chord. What you need to remember is that when the diminished chord is used as a substitute for a dom7 chord, it is one ½ step, or one fret, above the dom7 chord. For example, a C7 uses a C#o7 chord, A7 uses a Bbo7 chord, F uses an F#o7, etc. The following example shows how to make diminished 7th substitute chords from the dom7 chords we already know.

Ex. 18   Creating o7 chords from dom7 chords

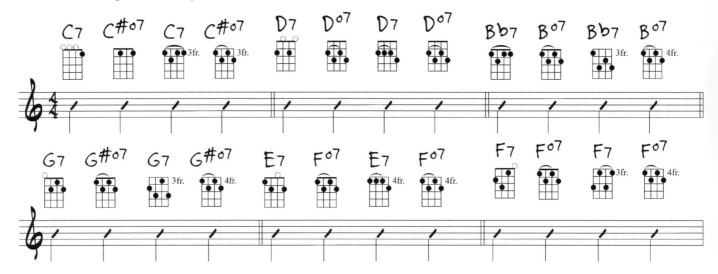

We'll see more examples of using the diminished 7th chord later in the book. In the meantime, go back to any of your favorite songs or progressions and substitute a diminished chord for the dom7 chords. The first you'll probably notice is that it doesn't always sound good. Some of that is just getting used to the sound of the diminished chord and some of it is because, well, it just doesn't sound good in every situation. However, sometimes it will sound *just right*. Because the diminished chord has such a distinctive sound, you need to be careful about where you use it and make sure it fits the music.

CHAPTER 3 - THE JAZZIER SIDE OF THINGS

First, let's be clear that this is not a book specifically about "jazz" ukulele. In fact, the chord progressions and examples in this section can be used in a variety of styles other than jazz – rock, pop, country, etc. However, when some musicians think about jazz, it often means "making something more complicated". Take the common phrase "to jazz something up" – it means to make something spicier or busier or faster or more colorful. For our purposes right now, it means to make our common chords a little more complex and to use substitutions to make chord progressions more complex as well. It also involves an element of improvising, which means we're not sticking to specific written-out chords, but we're making up music on the spot within a certain set of rules.

VAMPS

Let's start with the simplest of chord progressions – the two-chord vamp. A vamp is a melody, rhythm or progression (or a combination of all three) that is repeated an unlimited number of times, usually with another musician soloing over the vamp. Two-chord vamps are a fun way to start playing around with 7th chords and improvising because, well, it's hard to get lost, right? There are only two chords, so you always know what the next chord is. And because the vamp is repeated over and over, it's a good way make use of all the different chord positions you've been learning.

The first example is THE classic 70's-soft-rock vamp – the Imaj7 to the IVmaj7. It's about as mellow and laid-back as you can get, but it can be fun to play.

> **NOTE**: Just a reminder that even though these examples use 7th chords, you can also practice them with just plain major and minor chords. You should play around with both ways.

Ex. 19   *Imaj7 - IVmaj7 vamp*

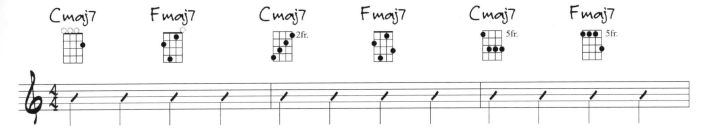

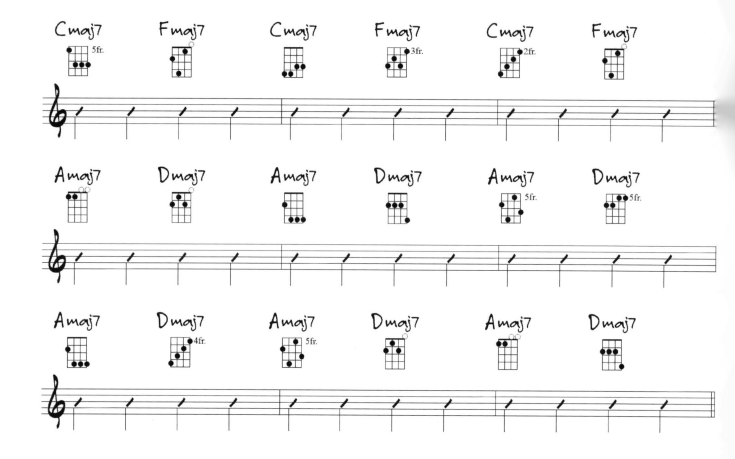

The next example also uses two maj7 chords but it's not quite as mellow.

Ex. 20   Imaj7 - bVIImaj7 vamp

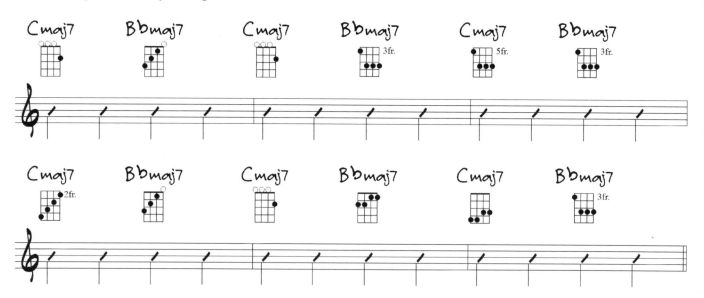

- 35 -

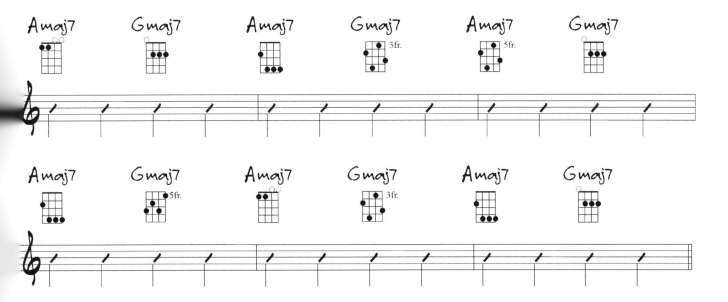

This next vamp uses a more abrupt chord change, going from the Imaj7 chord to the bIIImaj7 chord. It creates a darker sound, and has some interesting voice leading that you'll hear when moving around the different positions.

Ex. 21   *Imaj7 - bIIImaj7 vamp*

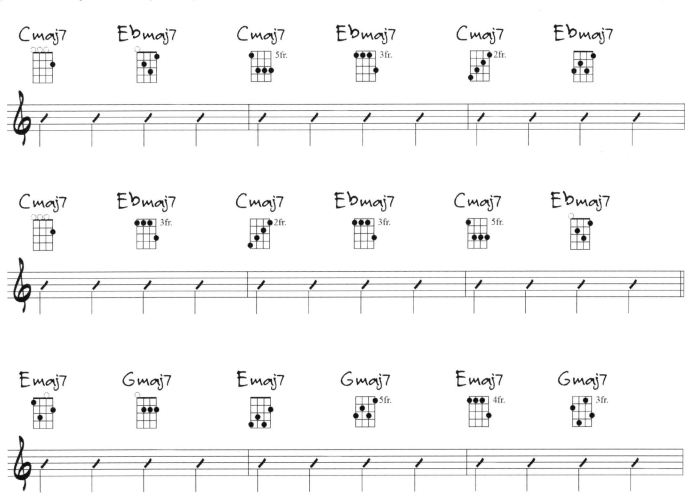

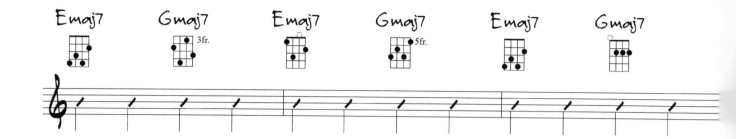

Next are some vamps that start on a min7 chord. The first one is a classic rock and blues vamp.

Ex. 22   Imin7 - IV7 vamp

- 37 -

The next example makes a nice minor vamp. Going to the bIImaj7 chord from the minor chord creates a nice "unsettled" feel.

Ex. 23   *Imin7 - bIImaj7 vamp*

The last example is a vamp that is really just one chord. The movement from the Imin7 chord to the IImin7 chord doesn't create a lot of movement or tension but tends to just decorate and embellish the Imin7 harmony. Everyone knows this as the "Moondance" vamp.

Ex. 24 *Imin7 - IImin7 vamp*

These are just some ideas to get you thinking about vamps, chord inversions, and moving around the neck. Take some time to make up your own vamp ideas. They don't have to be limited to two chords – they can be three or four chords, use different rhythms, or different combinations of major, minor, dom7, maj7, min7, and diminished chords.

TIP: As you connect the chords in your vamps, keep an ear open for melodies that will start to emerge on the top string.

PASSING CHORDS

Another way to embellish chords and progressions is the use of passing chords. As the name implies, these are connecting chords that you "pass through" from one chord to the next, usually chords of the same type. For example, if you're playing a measure of Cmaj7, you can play

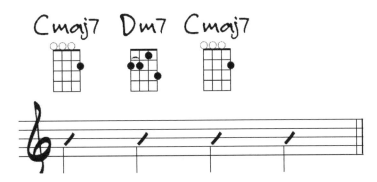

The Dmin7 temporarily steps away from the Cmaj7 sound and then returns, emphasizing the Cmaj7 harmony – you are in C major but you "pass through" D minor along the way. For songs where you play one chord for several measures, passing chords can add some interesting movement and energy.

- Passing chords are usually the IImin7 chord, the V7 chord, or a diminished chord. These are the examples we'll look at in this section.
- The primary chord should be played on the strong beats (beats 1 and 3), and the passing chord played on the weak beats (2 and 4). This helps to emphasize the primary chord.
- Be careful not to overuse passing chords. If you use them too much, you lose the sound of the original harmony because you're just jumping in and out instead of emphasizing the original harmony.
- On the other hand, for those times when you just don't know what to practice, a one-chord vamp can be a great way to get motivated. Just pick a key, say D minor, and start connecting chords around the neck with different passing chords.

Following are examples for three types of passing chords: minor, dominant, and diminished.

NOTE: Without diving into too much music theory, notice that all three types of passing chords are really functioning as a dominant chord: the IIm7 has a suspended sound (see Chapter 6), and the diminished chord has a flatted 9th sound (see Chapter 2).

The Passing Minor Chord

Let's start with the minor passing chord. This is the smoothest of our three types of passing chords. Note that this works well as a passing chord between major, minor and dominant chords.

Ex. 25   I - ii passing chord

Here are some examples of the passing chord as a minor 7th.

Ex. 26   I - IImin7 passing chord

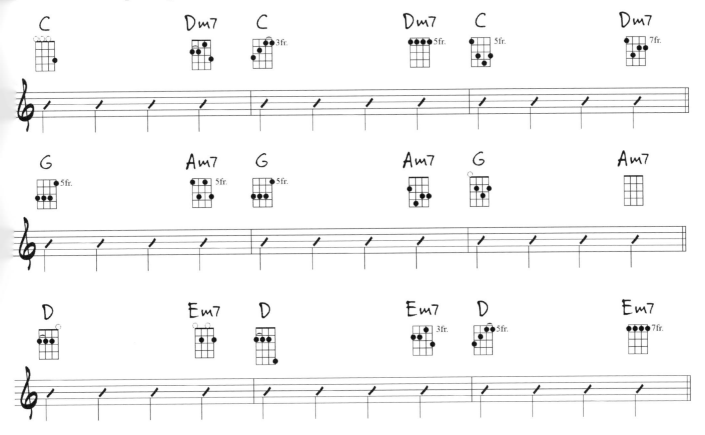

And some examples with the I chord as a major 7th.

Ex. 27   Imaj7 - IImin7 passing chord

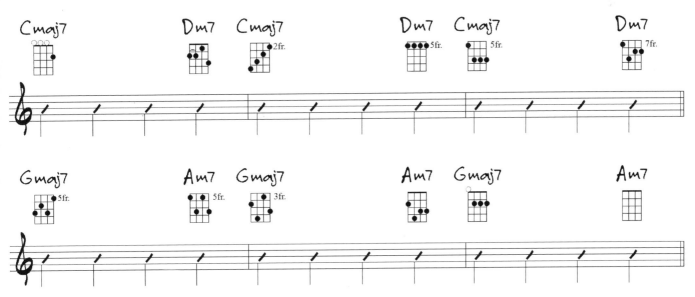

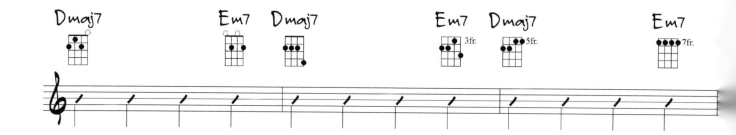

Passing chords also work when the I chord is a dom 7th.

Ex. 28 I7 - IImin7 passing chord

And some examples of when the I chord is a minor 7th.

Ex. 29   Imin7 - IImin7 passing chord

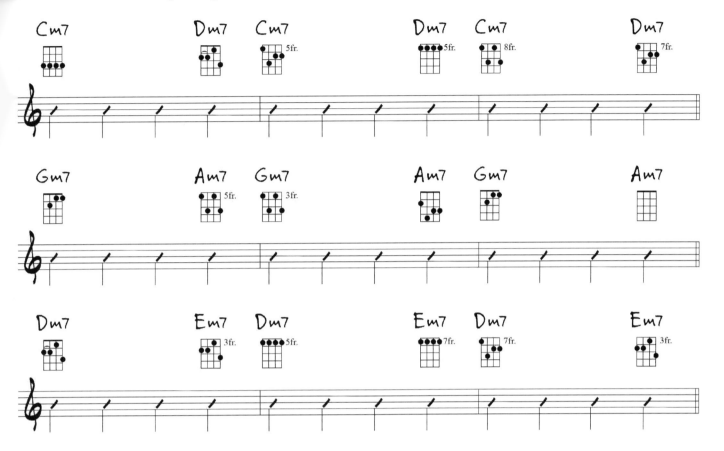

The passing dominant chord

Next is the V7 passing chord. Notice that the feeling of "stepping out" of the key is stronger with the V7 chord.

Ex. 30   I - V7 passing chord

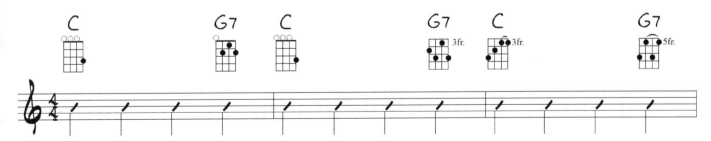

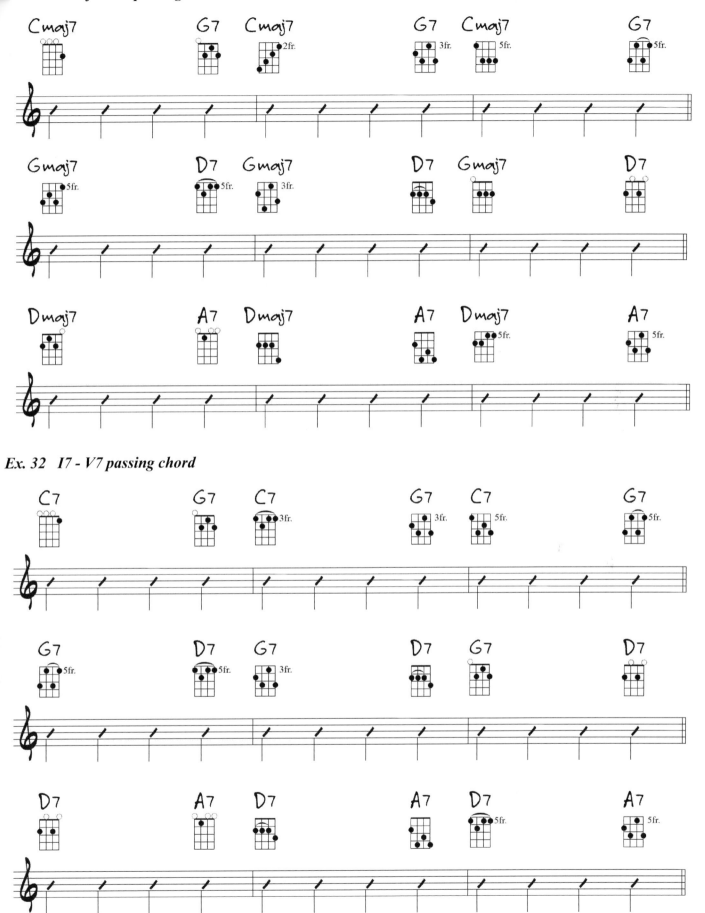

Ex. 33 Imin7 - V7 passing chord

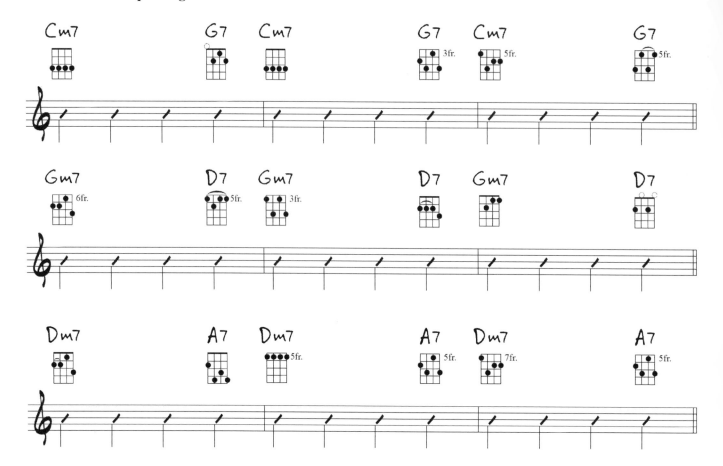

The Passing Diminished Chord

Finally, the diminished passing chord, which is really an extension of the V7 chord. However, the nature of the diminished chord creates much more tension and movement than a regular V7 chord. Remember from Chapter 2 that a diminished chord has four different names, so a substitute for a G7 could be Bdim7, Ddim7, Fdim7 or Abdim7.

Ex. 34 I - dim7 passing chord

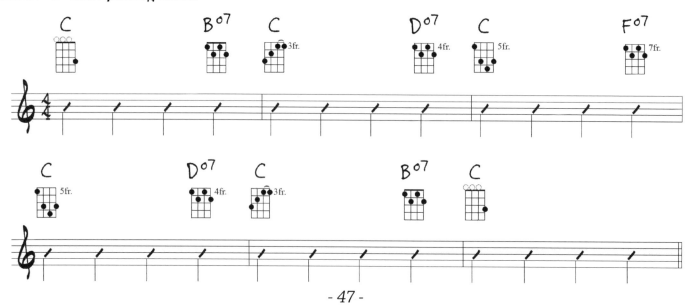

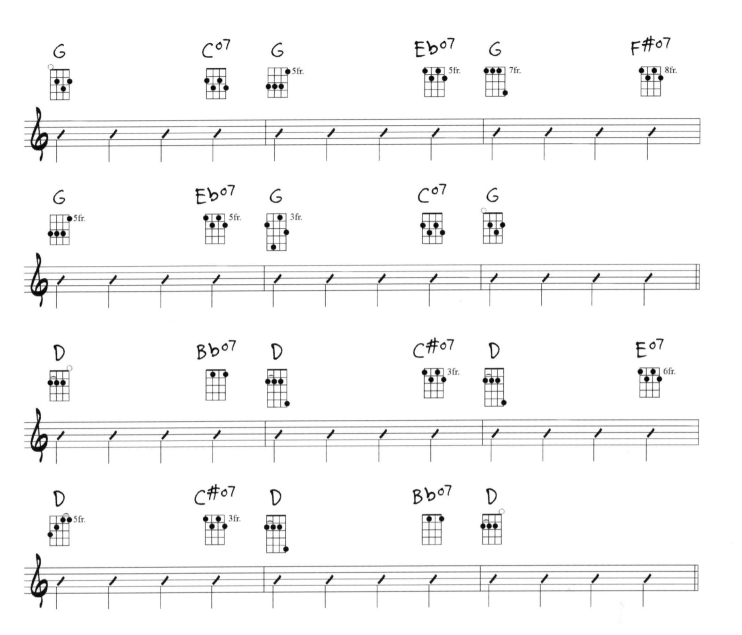

Ex. 35 Imaj7 - dim7 passing chord

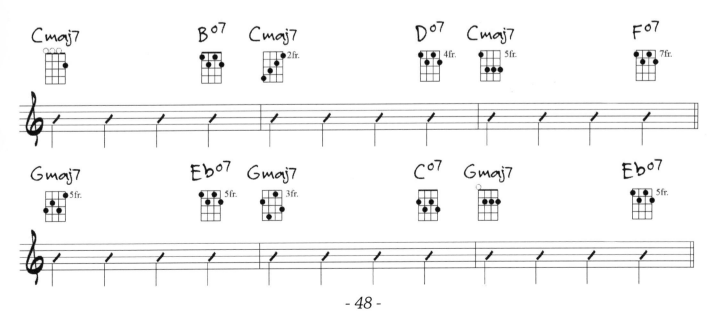

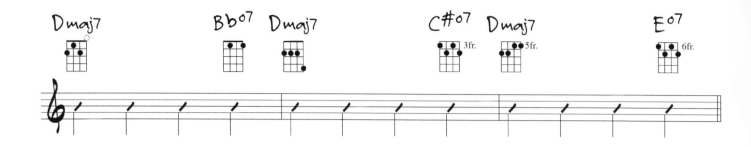

Ex. 36 I7 - dim7 passing chord

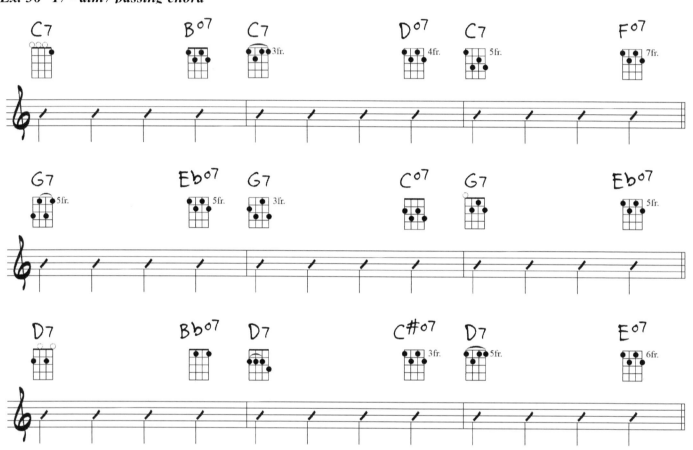

Ex. 37 Imin7 - dim7 passing chord

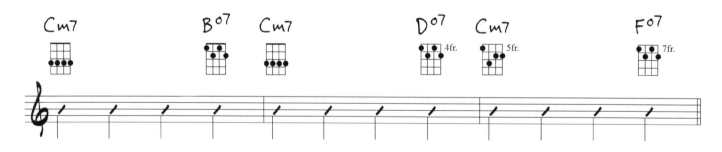

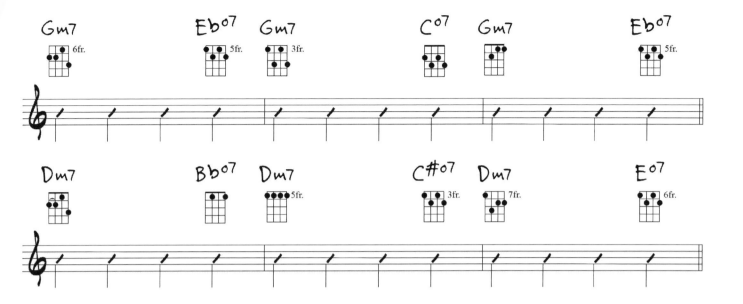

Now go back to some songs that you normally play and see where you can insert some passing chords. Sometimes they will work and sometimes they won't – let your ear be your guide. If you start to put them in everywhere, you'll soon hear for yourself where they work and where they don't.

NOTE: Just like with the vamps, keep an ear out for melodies that you create when connecting the chords.

CYCLES

In the last section on passing chords, I'm sure you noticed that moving away from the original chord created a tension that wanted to go back to the original chord again. For example, playing in C major and then playing G7 creates a tension, or a "pull", back to C major. This is because G has a **fifth** relationship to C [C=1, D=2, E=3, F=4, G=5, remember?] and in Western music the fifth has a strong desire to resolve that tension back to the home key.

So, if G is the fifth of C and wants to resolve to C, what if we added something before the G that wanted to resolve to G? Well, that would be the fifth of G, or D [G=1, A=2, B=3, C=4, D=5]. Try this:

1. Play two measures of C: || C / / / || C / / / ||
2. Now add a passing G: || C / / G || C / / / ||
3. Now add a D before the G: || C / D G || C / / / ||

We can continue this process by adding the fifth of D (which would be A) before the D to create:

|| C A D G || C / / / ||

Now we have the A resolving to the D, which resolves to G, which in turn resolves back to C. This process of one chord resolving to another, then becoming the fifth of the next chord and resolving to that one, etc., is called the **cycle**.

- 50 -

Note: Technically, it's called the **cycle of fifths** or **circle of fifths**, and if you keep resolving to the next chord (C to F, F to Bb, Bb to Eb, etc.) you go through all 12 keys and wind up where you started, and the cycle starts all over again (hence the "circle of fifths"). Google "circle of fifths" and you'll find plenty of information.

Cycles are used in some fashion in all music and are very common in jazz. For our purposes, we're only going to use short sections of the cycle to embellish our progressions.

The first example is the most common cycle in jazz and a lot of 50's and 60's pop tunes.

Ex. 38 Cycle: Imaj7 – VImin7 – IImin7 – V7

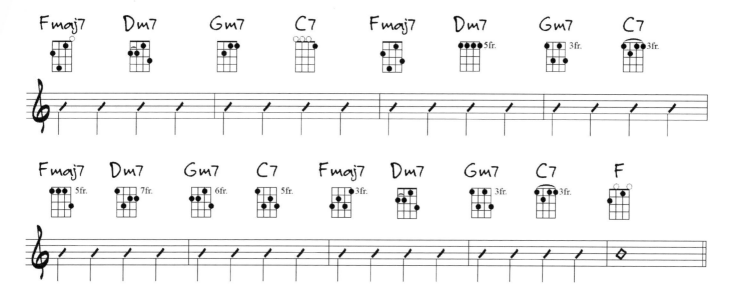

The next example is a variation of the last one, replacing the Imaj7 chord with the IIImin7, and the VImin7 with the VI7.

Ex. 39 Cycle: IIImin7 – VI7 – IImin7 – V7

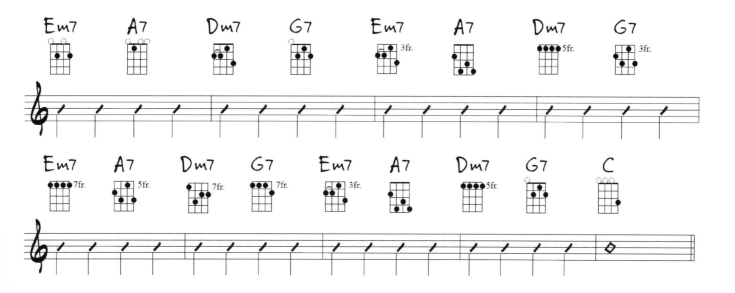

The last example is another variation, but we replace the VI7 chord with the chromatic passing chord between the IIImin7 and the IImin7.

NOTE: We didn't discuss chromatic passing chords in the **Passing Chords** section, but they are a very handy trick that most people figure out on their own eventually. When moving between two chords that use the same form, just slide the whole thing down one fret and it usually works.

Ex. 40 Cycle: IIImin7 – bIIImin7 – IImin7 – V7

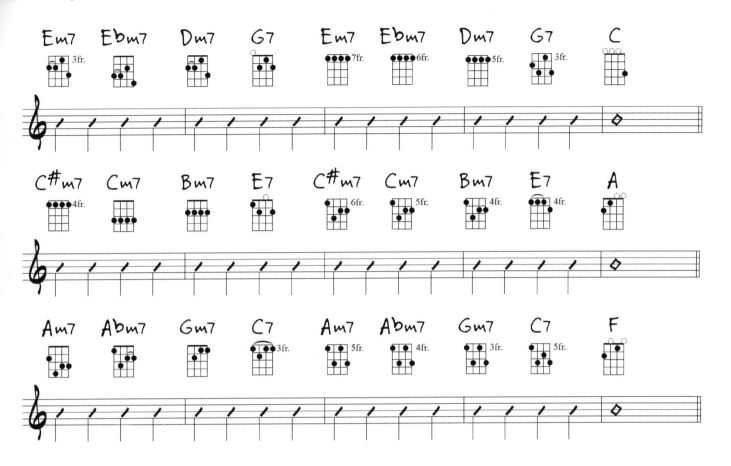

PASSING CHORDS AND CYCLES IN PROGRESSIONS

Now let's apply the passing chord and cycle techniques to some progressions.

The first progression is a basic 12-bar blues. The blues form is great for experimenting with because it's common to rock, country, and jazz music and the structure lends itself to a million different variations.

As a refresher, here's the very basic blues form, just consisting of the I7, IV7, and V7 chords.

Blues: Basic form

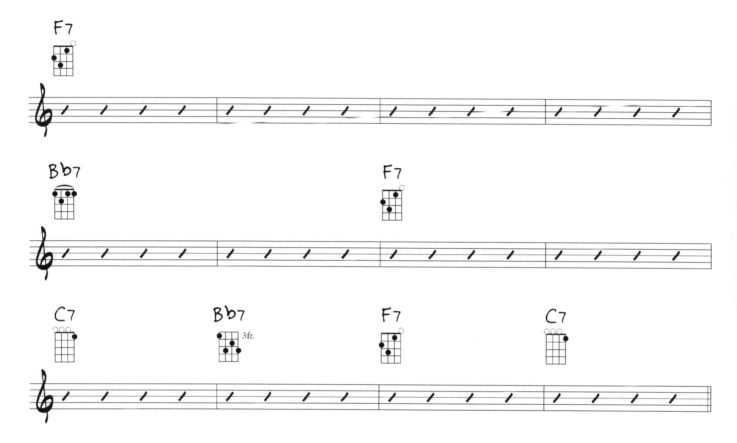

Now, let's start dressing it up.

> **NOTE**: I have annotated the variations with the "how" and "why" of the different substitutions. While it would benefit you to read through and see what's happening musically, if this kind of theoretical stuff bores you, please just play through the variations. The important thing is to hear the sounds and get them under your fingers.

Blues: Variation 1

Measure 2: Instead of staying on the F7 for four measures, this Bb7 chord works as a passing chord to add some movement to the song. The F7 to Bb7 also makes a good vamp to play around with.

Measure 4: Here we can take advantage of a short cycle to get to the Bb7 chord in measure 5. Notice that all we did was add the Cmin7 chord, but that wants to resolve to the F7, which in turn emphasizes the resolution to the Bb7.

Measures 8-10: This is a common cycle substitution in the blues. It's best to start by looking at it backwards. We want to create a cycle to the C7 chord measure 9, so we put a Gm7 before the C7. To make room for this, we get rid of the Bb7 in measure 10 and move the C7 to measure 10 and add the Gm7 to measure 9. Then, we add a D7 to measure 8 that resolves to the Gm7.

Measures 11-12: These two measures are called the "turnaround", which is the resolution at the end of a song that creates some movement to "turn" the progression around to the beginning again. We embellish the basic form with a passing Bb7 for two beats, then back to the F7 and C7.

Ex. 41 Blues variation 1

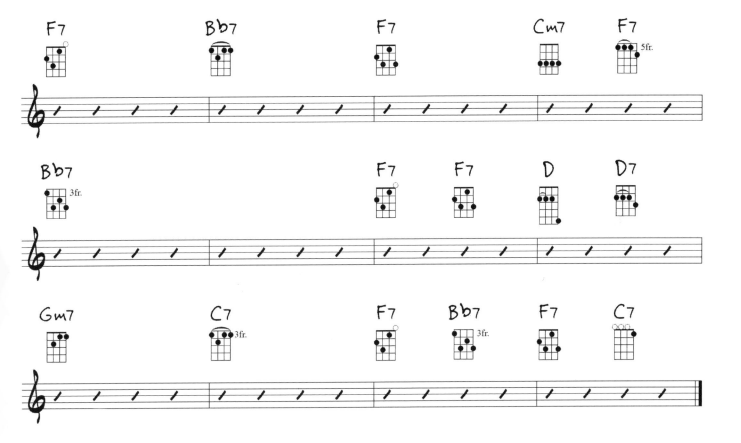

Blues: Variation 2

Measures 2-4: In measure 2, we start a longer cycle that takes us all the way to the Bb7 chord in measure 5. This is a common cycle substitution in jazz and bebop songs. (I wouldn't advise trying to force it into a traditional blues jam.)

Measure 6: Instead of repeating the Bb7, we create some tension by substituting a B diminished 7th chord. This is another common substitution that can be used in most all blues types.

Measures 7-8: These measures add some passing chords that lead to the Gm7 in measure 9. In measure 7, we start on F7 and pass through Gm7. However, in measure 8 we don't go back to F7, but keep going up instead to Am7, and then use a chromatic passing chord to get to the Gm7 in measure 9.

Remember that in Variation 1 we used a D7 in measure 8. In this variation, the Am7 can also be thought of as leading into that D7 – in other words, these measures could also be || F / / / || Am7 / D7 / ||. Then we add the Gm7 passing chord and replace the D7 with the Abm7 chromatic passing chord. As you start playing more with substitutions and passing chords, you'll find that there several ways to explain the same thing.`

Measure 6: Instead of repeating the Bb7, we create some tension by substituting a B diminished 7th chord. This is another common substitution that can be used in most all blues types.

Ex. 42 Blues variation 2

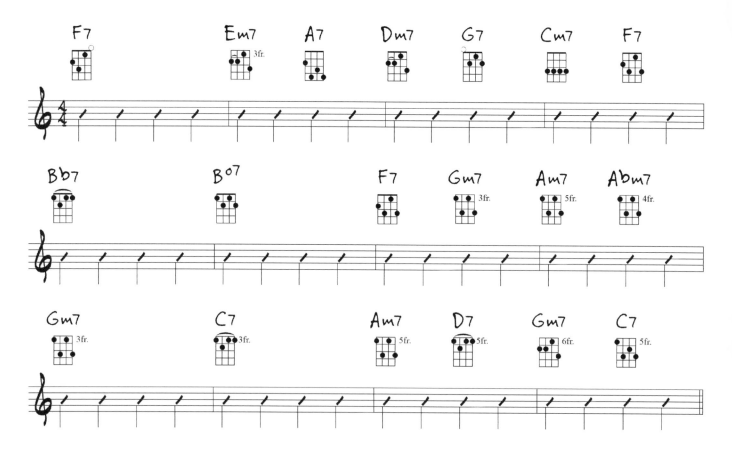

Blues: Variation 3

Measures 1-4: We start with the same long cycle as Variation 2 but use chromatic passing chords to get to the Bb7 in measure 5.

Measure 6: Instead of the diminished chord from Variation 2, we use the Bbm7 chord here. Notice how it leads nicely to the Am7 in measure 7.

Measures 7-8: This is an interesting use of chromatic passing chords. We're using the Am7 - D7 idea from the last variation but compressing it to one measure and then moving both chords down chromatically one fret to get to the Gm7 chord in measure 9.

Measure 9: Uses a chromatic passing chord to the C7.

Measures 11-12: This is the same turnaround as Variation 2, but with some chromatic passing chords.

Ex. 43 Blues variation 3

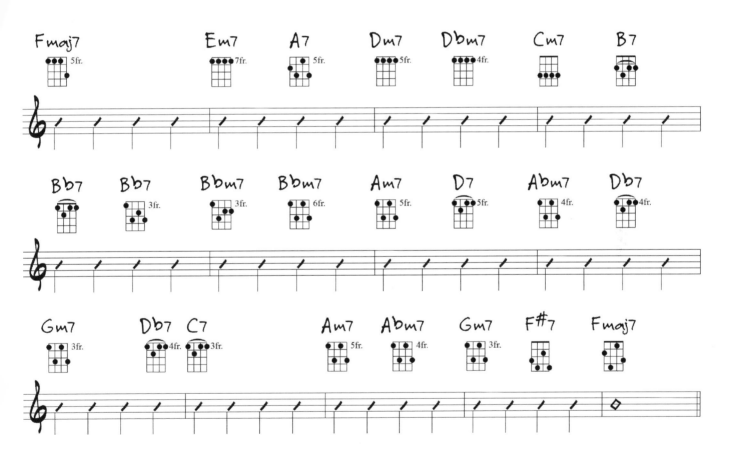

So, our three variations have a lot going on, but don't stop there – take these ideas and the techniques you've learned so far to improvise new variations. Use passing chords, cycles, different positions, add 7ths or don't use 7ths at all, use all minor chords, simplify all the chords or play a different chord on each beat – just experiment and listen for sounds that SOUND GOOD TO YOU. Be sure and write down any ideas that you like so you don't forget them!

Rhythm Changes

The second progression that we'll look at is what is know as Rhythm Changes. The progression is used in hundreds of jazz songs but takes its name from George Gershwin's song "I Got Rhythm". The form is a standard AABA form, meaning that there is an 8-measure section (A) that is repeated, then an 8-measure bridge (B) and then the A section is repeated again.

The basic form already uses plenty of cycles and passing chords, so we'll just point out a few of the highlights in the A sections and then look at some variations of the bridge.

Measures 1-4: A basic I-VI-ii-V cycle, followed by a iii-VI-ii-V cycle

Measure 5: This measure emphasizes a Bb7 that leads to the Eb7 in measure 6.

Measure 6: The Eb7 – Eo7 leads back to the Bb chord (or a turnaround in this case). Sometimes an Ebm7 is used instead of the Eo7, as we saw in the blues Variation 3.

Measures 7-8: In the very basic rhythm changes form, these measures are just Bb and F7, but are usually replaced with a cycle.

Measure 9: Using the Bo7 instead of the G7 is a standard substitution.

Measures 17-24: This is the B section, or the bridge. In its basic form, it's just a cycle of all dominant 7th chords, two measures each, that lead back to the Bb in measure 25 when the A section repeats again. Because there is so much space between the chords, the bridge is usually subjected to lots of variations and substitutions.

Measures 25-32: This is a repeat of the A section, with one chromatic passing chord thrown in.

Ex. 44 Rhythm changes: Basic form

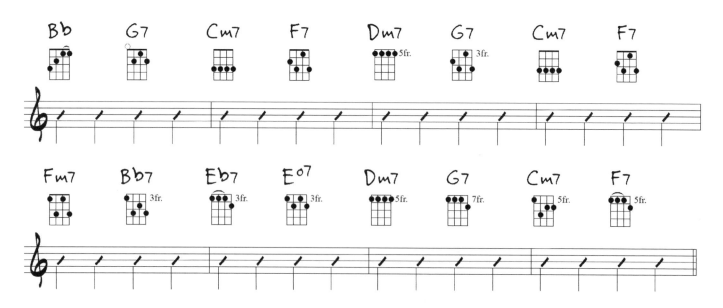

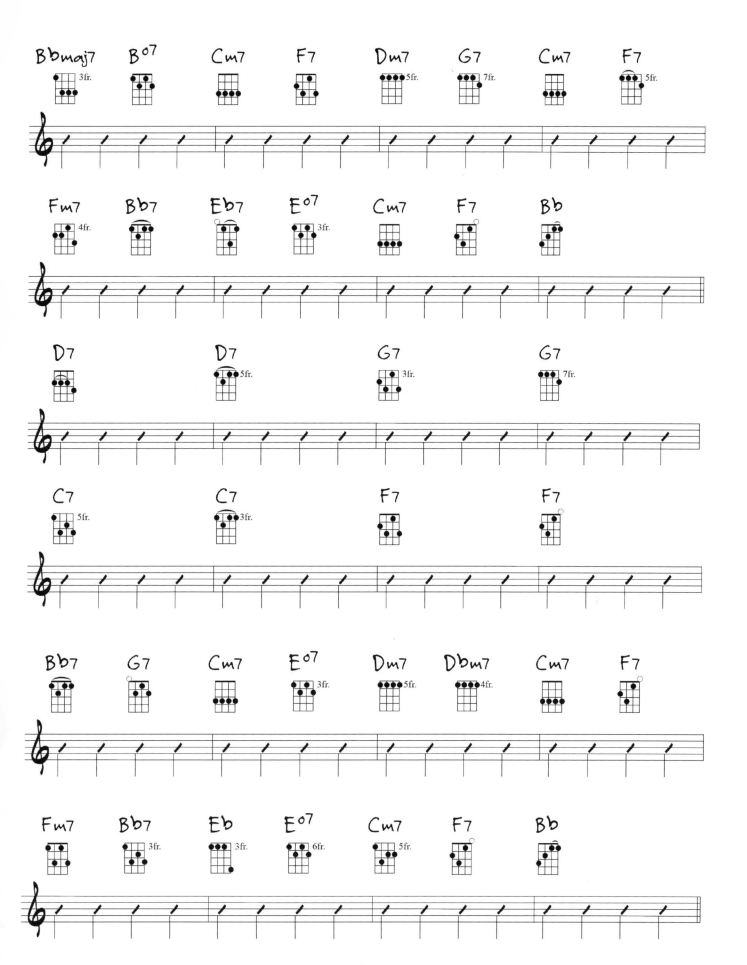

Now let's look at some variations for the bridge.

The first variation just adds a minor 7th chord before each dominant chord, which adds a little more movement and interest than the plain dominant chords. This is the standard way that rhythm changes are played at most jazz jam sessions.

The second variation adds some extra passing chords and cycles. I'm not sure I would throw in all of these at once in performance situation, but there are plenty of good ideas to use.

Measures 9-10: The A7 is a passing chord between the D7, and the Ab7 is a chromatic passing chord to the G7

Measure 11-12: Notice that these two measures are a repeat of the previous two measures, but just in a different key. The D7 is a passing chord, and the Db7 leads to the C7. Repeating the same chord substitutions (although not necessarily the same voicings or inversions, in this case) is a common way to repeat a musical idea and tie the song together.

Measure 14: This uses a cycle that leads up to a chromatic passing chord, the Gb7, to get to the F7. It sounds a little "outside" at first, but if you play it smoothly and focus on landing cleanly on the F7, it sounds pretty cool.

> As an extra credit workout, try playing some cycles like measure 14 up and down the neck, connecting different dom7th chord forms with one chord per beat. As long as you focus on the chord that you want to land on, sometimes you can lead up to it with pretty much any weird stuff you want to and get away with it.

Measure 15: This uses a diminished passing chord.

Measure 16: This uses a dominant 7th passing chord but then goes right to a chromatic passing chord to lead back to the Bb chord at the beginning.

Ex. 45 Rhythm changes: Bridge variations

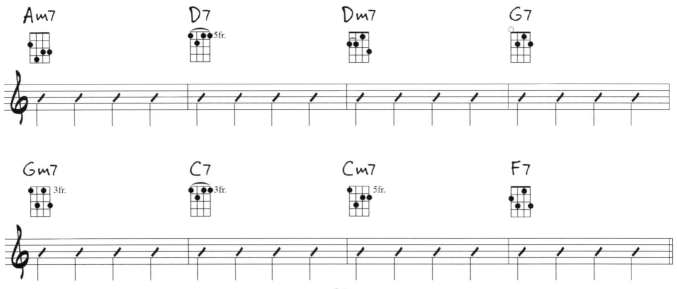

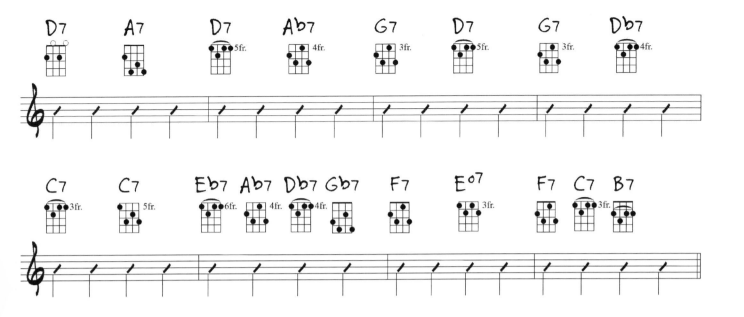

A FINAL WORD ON JAZZ CHORDS

As I mentioned at the beginning of this chapter, this isn't specifically about jazz ukulele. However, many of you who like jazz will no doubt find sheet music or chords for jazz songs and find that they are full of chords like G6/9, C7(#9), Amin9(11), etc. These can look intimidating, but the good thing is that you can use the knowledge you already have to fake your way through most jazz songs.

Pretty much every chord in every song, no matter how complicated, functions in one of three basic ways: as *major*, *minor*, or *dominant*. And you already know your major 7th chords, your minor 7th chords, and your dominant 7th chords, so you have the tools you need right there. The following chart shows how you can substitute chords you already know for all of those weird jazz chords.

NOTE: Of course, these substitutions won't sound as complex as the original chords, but they will function the same within the song.

For this type of chord:		Use this basic chord:
Major [Cmaj7 or CM7 or C∆7]		C major or Cmaj7
• C6 • C6/9 • Cmaj7 • Cmaj9	• Cadd 9 • Cmaj7(#11) • Cmaj13	
Minor [Cmin7 or Cm7 or C-7]		C minor or Cmin7
• Cmin6 • Cmin7 • Cmin9	• Cmin11 • Cmin13 • Cm6/9	
Cmin7(b5) is a special case, see the next table.		
Dominant [C7 or Cdom7]		C7
• C7 • C9 • C13	• C7(b9) • C7(#9) • C7(b13)	
C7(b5) is a special case, see the next table.		

There are a few other common jazz chords that you'll run across that require a little math to figure out the conversion. The next chart explains some of the shortcuts.

For this type of chord:	Use this type of chord:
Cmin7(b5)	Eb minor or Ebm7 The min7(b5) chord is common in minor key jazz progressions. As a substitute for the min7(b5), you can use a minor chord that is three 1/2 steps (or three frets) up from the original chord.
C7(b5)	F#7 The 7(b5) chord has a pretty unique sound (listen to the second chord in "Take the A Train"). The substitute chord is a 7th chord six 1/2 steps (or six frets) away (also known as the tritone).
C7b9	C#o7 (or Eo7 or Go7 or Bbo7) We touched on this in the section on diminished chords. The easiest way to remember this is to use a diminished chord ½ step (or one fret) above the root of the chord.

That's it for passing chords and cycles. Practice different ways to incorporate them into your playing and they can add a lot of interest and excitement and enhance the music. But be careful to only use them where they serve the music. Remember the Golden Rule of Ukulele:

Sometimes all you need is a C major chord.

CHAPTER 4 - CREATING CHORD MELODIES

Sometimes when you're accompanying another singer (or yourself), you'll need to play a little bit of the melody so the singer (or you) can hear the starting notes. Or maybe you don't sing and just want to play the melody of a song with some chord accompaniment. Or perhaps you just want to play some short licks to fill in between lyrics. All of these involve playing what is commonly called "chord melody" style. All that means is that you're emphasizing a melody, or some melodic line, on the top strings (usually the first string, but often using the second string) while playing some supporting chords underneath.

With what you've learned so far about different chord inversions, vamps, and passing chords, you've got a good foundation for adding melodies to your playing. In this section, we'll look at how to add melodies to single chords and vamps, how to connect melodies and chords up and down the neck, and finally how to make a chord melody arrangement of a simple song.

EXTENDING SINGLE CHORDS

Let's start with some basic open string chords.

In the following examples, the basic chord is indicated with black dots and the extension notes are indicated by diamonds.

Ex. 1: Just a basic G chord.

Ex. 2: Using the barre form of the G chord allows you to reach farther up the neck.

Ex. 3: Notice in the 2nd measure that you are temporarily playing an F#min chord. This happens a lot when playing in this style – just think of them as "melodic passing chords".

Ex. 4: When playing a C chord with the bottom three strings open, you can actually fret notes on the first string all the way up until you run out of frets. Play around with this idea and see what melodies you can figure out.

Ex. 5: This example uses extensions notes on the second string. Notice how the sound of this is a little more subtle because the highest note isn't moving. In the next chapter we'll explore more "moving inside lines" like this.

Ex. 6: Another moving inside line and a "must know" rock'n'roll riff.

Ex. 7: This can be a little tricky to play both the open string and the 5th fret while playing the bottom three strings smoothly.

Ex 8: This is a good stretch to be able to add to an F chord.

Ex. 46 *Chord melody: open position chords*

Now let's look at some closed position chord forms.

Ex. 9: This adds a line on the second string and then continues it on the first string. To emphasize the line even more, you can mute the first string or not play it on the first two beats.

Ex. 10: This a very useful little vamp. The trick is to use one finger (I use my third finger) to fret the bottom three strings, and then flatten down that same finger to get all four strings.

Ex. 11: This is another example of a line moving from the first string down to the second string.

Ex. 12: This is a nice way to embellish a minor chord. The tricky part is flattening your little finger to get the 5th fret on the last beat.

Ex. 47 Chord melody: closed position chords

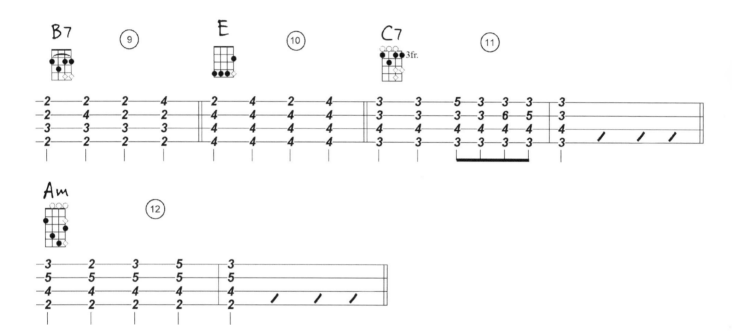

Let's put them together into a simple progression. The first example is in B major and the second example is in B minor. Notice how similar they are to each other – the notes in the chords and the extension notes only have one or two frets difference.

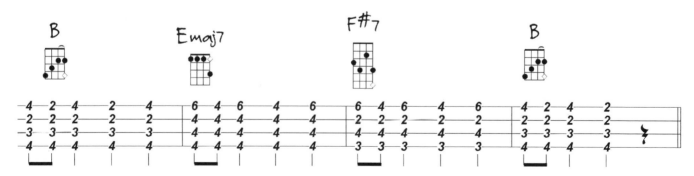

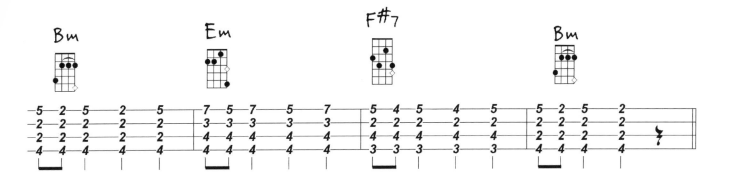

USING EXTENSIONS TO CONNECT CHORDS

When we learned closed position chords and vamps, we started to see how we connect chords up and down the neck. Now we can add extension notes to chords to make those transitions smoother and start creating melodies.

NOTE: In these examples, I've only indicated the basic chord in the chord grid. The extension notes are indicated in the tab.

Let's start with a few examples connecting different forms of one chord. When playing extension notes, hold down the chord for as long as you can before moving to the next chord. This helps create a full sound of a cord and melody being played at the same time.

Ex. 48 Connecting one chord

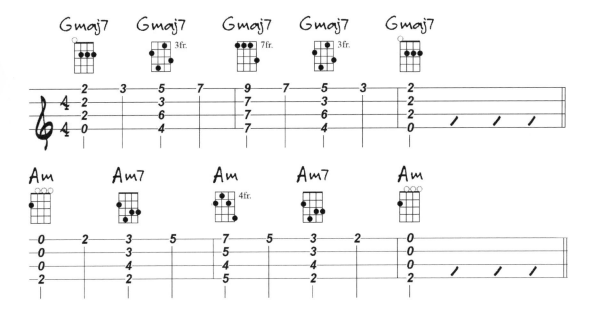

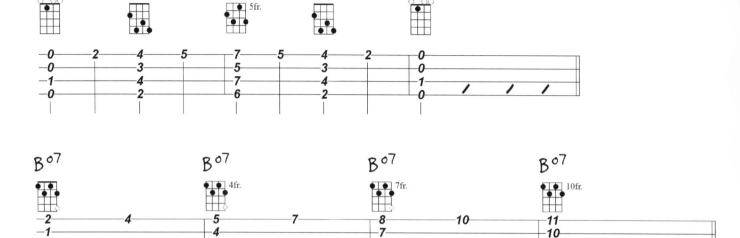

This next example shows how you can connect two chords with a variety of different extension patterns and some shifting. These are all variations on our basic IImin7 – V7 vamp.

Some things to watch out for:

Var. 4: Stretch your little finger up to the 5th fret while holding down the F chord so it continues to sound. The more flexible your little finger gets the more extension notes you'll be able to reach.

Var. 5: Flatten your first finger to get the 1st fret while still holding down the F chord.

Var. 12: Notice that both chords start with an extension note as part of the chord. Sometimes this is necessary to accommodate a melody.

Var. 13: This is an example of using a "sequence". In music, a sequence is a melody or musical phrase whose basic pattern is repeated over a different harmony, or chord.

Var. 14 and 15: These examples shift up to a different F chord.

Ex. 49 *Connecting two chords*

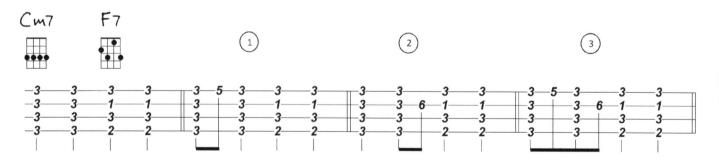

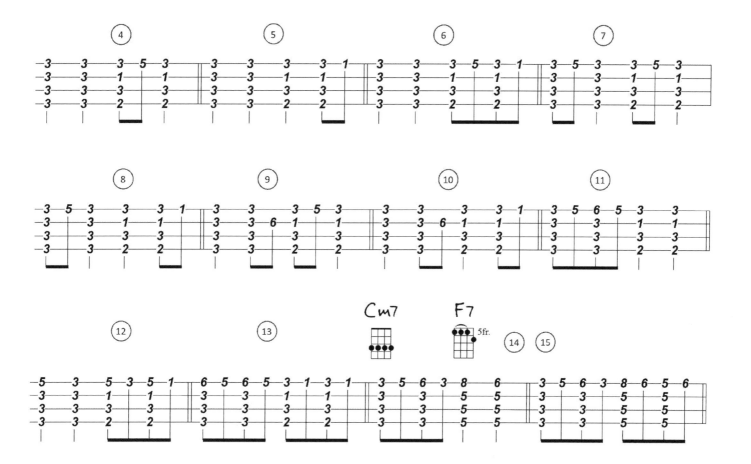

For practice, go back and try this on some of the other vamps that you worked on earlier. See where you can add interesting extensions and start to pick out melodies. Be sure to write down any interesting ideas you stumble across so you can add them to your own bag of riffs.

Now, let's take a jazzier example using a cycle, or turnaround, in the key of F.

Var. 1: This uses very basic connecting notes.

Var. 2: This variation uses a trick that is unique to string instruments – alternating with an open string. This doesn't always work with every chord in every key, but fortunately it works well in this example.

Var. 3: This example uses a more chromatic approach to build a descending melody. Notice that this is also a sequence, with the top melody repeated over different chords.

Var. 4: This variation uses some jazz alterations on the D7 and C7 chords. It can be very pretty used in a ballad.

Var. 5: This example pulls out all the stops and uses a chromatic line and jazz alterations in a sequence. In cases like this where your melody line gets very busy or complex, it's going to be harder to hold down and sustain the underlying chord. That's okay, though, because the focus will be on the melody line.

Ex. 50 Turnaround connections

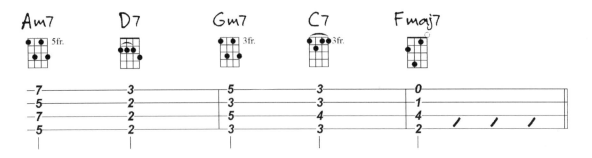

Var. 1

Var. 2

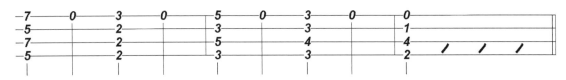

Var. 3

Var. 4

Var. 5

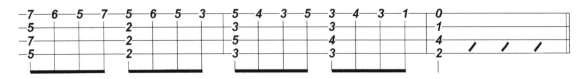

MAKING YOUR OWN CHORD MELODY ARRANGEMENTS

Finally, let's put all this together into an actual song where you'll play the chords and the melody together. This is an arrangement of a simple tune, "You Are My Sunshine". It uses chords you should already know along with some basic connection notes.

Ex. 51 Chord melody example

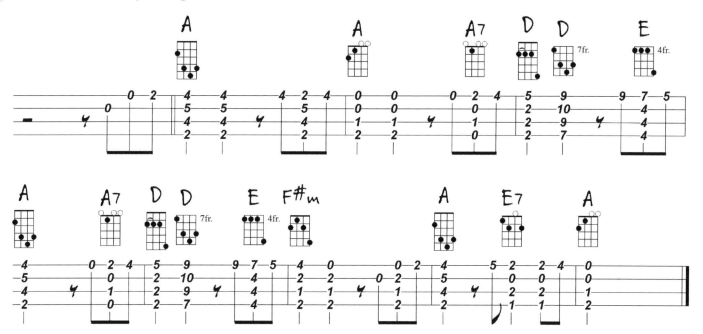

If you've studied everything in the book up to now, you have the basic skills to create your own chord melody song arrangements. Start with simple melodies and songs that you know and stick to basic chords. Once you have a basic arrangement structure, then you can add 7th chords, passing chords, etc. to make it your own. Here are some general tips for creating chord melody arrangements:

- Figure out the melody first. Try to keep most of the melody on the first string. This might mean moving the song to a different key, but it will make it easier to match full chords to the melody.
- If any of the melody falls on the second string be sure to mute the first string so the melody is emphasized.
- Don't try to play one chord for every melody note. That's why we learned extension notes, so you can play a chord and let it sustain while you add melody notes on top.
- In general, play chords on the beat, that is on 1, 2, 3, or 4, even if the melody is not part of the chord. Notice in in measures 1 and 2 of the previous song example, the last chords are right on beat 4, but the melody is an extension of the basic chord. Putting the chords on the beats keeps the rhythm flowing.

CHAPTER 5 – MOVING LINES

So far, we've looked at a couple of different ways to embellish situations where you're playing one chord for several measures. You can use different inversions, or passing chords, or chord extensions in the melody, etc. Another method you can use are chords with moving lines. These are chords that you already know, but one of the notes in the chord moves up or down, creating movement over (or under, or through) the chord. The moving line can appear on any of the strings. Many of them are common musical clichés, and I'm sure you'll recognize them.

All the examples start with a basic major or minor chord and then create other types of chords as the lines move up or down. Our first example introduces a new chord type – the 6th chord. Just as 7th chords are built using the 1, 3, 5, and 7 notes, a 6th chord is built using the 1, 3, 5, and 6.

NOTE: You may recognize that the Cmaj6 chord is the same chord form as an Amin7 chord. In fact, they share the same notes – C, E, G, and A. These are known as chord homonyms – chords that sound the same but have different functions depending on the context.

The first example starts with a major chord and the moving descending line creates a maj7, then a dom7, then a maj6 chord. The next three examples shift the moving line to a different string.

Ex. 52 Moving lines with 7th chords

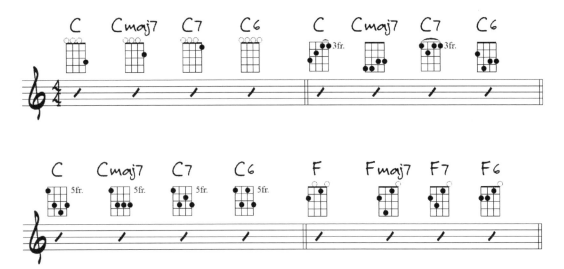

This example is similar to the last one, but the progression skips the dom7 chord and moves from the maj7 to the maj6 and then back again. As a repeating pattern, it works more like a vamp.

Ex. 53 Moving lines with major chords

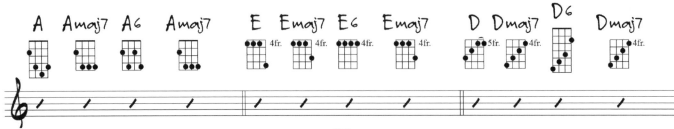

The next example is a classic moving-line vamp with a darker sound that creates a lot of movement, even though it really is just decorating one chord. The passing chord in the middle is an augmented chord, which is a basic major chord (1, 3, 5) with the 5th raised one half step. Like the diminished chord (Chapter 2), it has a unique sound and creates some tension as the line moves up and down.

Ex. 54 Moving lines with augmented chords

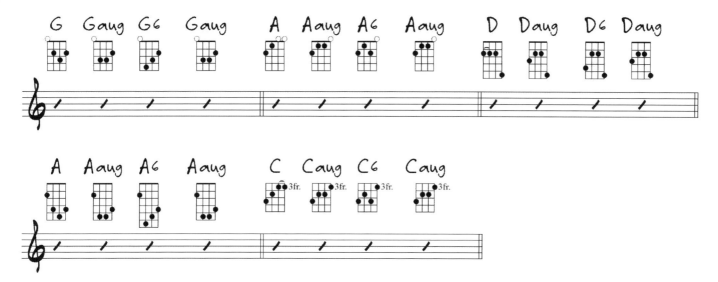

The same concepts above can be applied to minor chords as well. Here some examples in a few different keys.

NOTE: The minor(maj7) chord is another new chord type that you may not have seen before. It's created just like the maj7 chord that you already know, only with a minor chord. The sound, however, is quite different - where the maj7 chord has a pretty and restful sound, the minor(maj7) chord has a darker and unsettled sound.

Ex. 55 Moving lines with minor chords

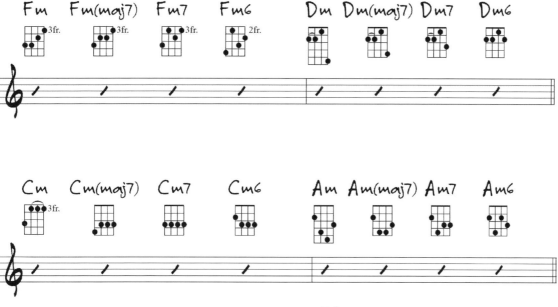

Ex. 56 *Moving lines with minor augmented chords*

The last example is the minor version of the major-augmented above. (I'm not sure why, but there is no "minor augmented" chord. However, there is a minor flat 6th chord (mb6) that is the same thing, just with a different name.

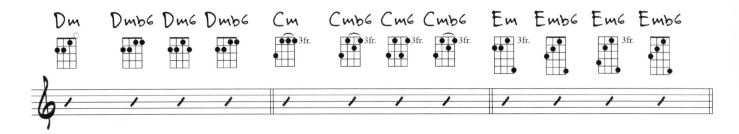

CHAPTER 6 - SUSPENDED CHORDS

Suspended chords, or **sus** chords, have a unique sound that you will recognize. Why are they suspended? Well, do you remember how chords are built on the 1, 3, and 5 of a scale? Suspended chords are built on the 1, 4, and 5. The 4th is *suspended* over the 3rd, and then usually resolves down to the 3rd (although not always – sometimes a suspended chord is just a suspended chord).

Take a look at this example. First play the D chord, then the Dsus, and then the D again. The suspended chord sounds like it's almost going to another chord, but not quite. This is another good option for creating some movement over a single chord. They work particularly well over vamps.

Ex. 57 Suspended chord example

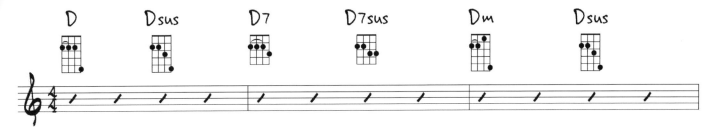

Did you notice in the that example that the suspended chord built from the major chord is the same as the one built from the minor chord? That's because we're not using the 3rd of the chord, and the 3rd is the note that determines whether the chord is major or minor. By replacing the 3rd with the 4th, you have neither a major nor minor chord, and that's why suspended chords have that vague, unsettled sound.

Here are some more examples of chord forms you already know and their related suspended versions.

Ex. 58 More suspended chord forms

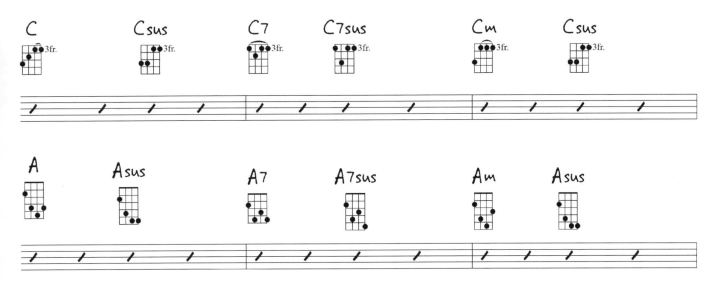

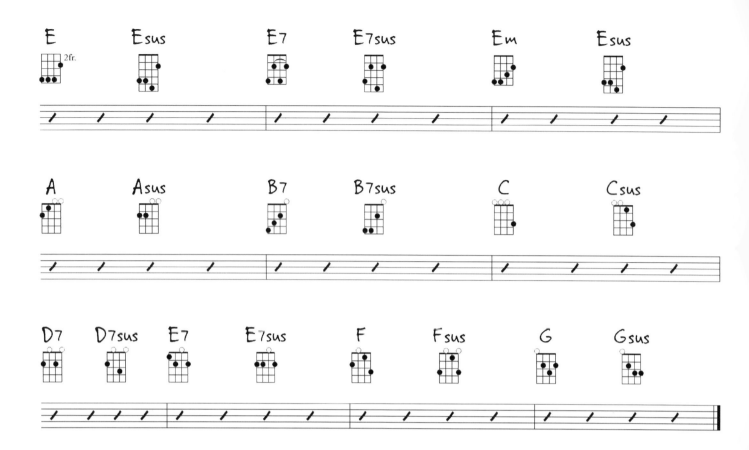

CHAPTER 7 - OKAY, JUST A LITTLE MORE JAZZ

To wrap up, let's look at some funkier jazz and blues chords. First, we'll look at dominant 9th and 13th chords, which can easily substitute for any dominant 7th chord. Then, we'll look at chords with an altered 9th and 13th, which can substitute for a V7 chord in many cases. Finally, we'll look at the 6/9 chord, a versatile chord shape that has a cool modern jazz sound.

9TH AND 13TH CHORDS

So, we know that there are seven notes in a scale and we use the 1st, 3rd, 5th and 7th to build chords. Then where do the 9th and 13th come from? We get them by just repeating the scale again and continuing the numbering, like this:

Key of C:	C	D	E	F	G	A	B	C	**D**	E	F	G	**A**	B
Scale degree:	1	2	3	4	5	6	7	8	**9**	10	11	12	**13**	14

So, if a 9th is the same note as the 2nd, and the 13th is the same note as the 6th, why isn't it called a 2nd chord or a 6th chord? The difference is <u>whether or not the the chord has a 7th in it</u>. For example, there is such a thing as a 6th chord, which is built using the 1st, 3rd, 5th and 6th. However, a 13th chord is build using the 1st, 3rd, 5th, 7th and 13th (and optionally a 9th). The same reasoning applies to the 9th and 2nd.

> **NOTE**: Extra notes added to a chord (that is, other than the 1, 3, 5, or 7) are called extensions. This is because they don't really change the basic type of the chord (major, minor or dominant), they just extend the quality of the sound. All the examples in this section are substitutes for dominant 7th chords, so they are dominant 9ths and 13ths. However, 9ths and 13ths also apply to major and minor chords as well.

Let's look at 9th and 13th chords over the following I7 VI7 II7 V7 progression:

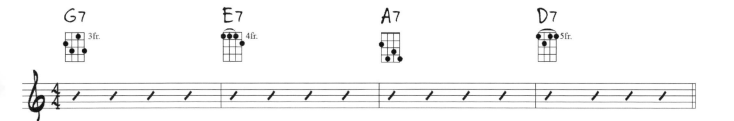

Let's add the 9th chord for each 7th chord shape.

Ex. 59 Dominant 9th chords

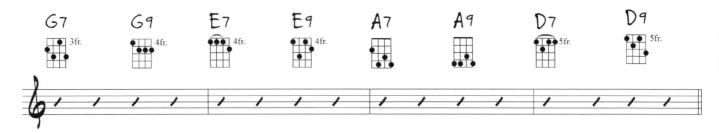

And then for the 13th chord (without the 9th).

Ex. 60 Dominant 13th chords

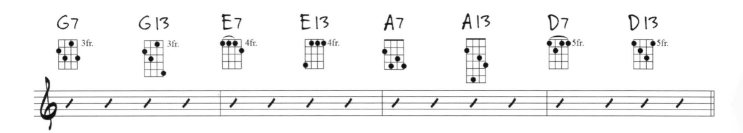

Now the 13th chord with the 9th. Listen for the slight difference in sound from the previous 13th shape.

Ex. 61 Dominant 13th chords with the 9th

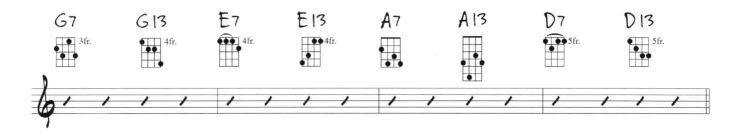

Finally, let's combine all the previous forms together. Listen for the different moving lines that are created from the chord shapes.

Ex. 62 Dominant 9th and 13th mixed

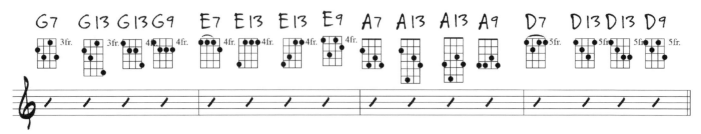

Here are two more variations mixing 7th, 9th and 13th shapes together in a more musical application.

Ex. 63 Dominant 9th and 13th mixed

Try substituting 9th and 13th chords for dominant 7th chords in songs that you already know. Some will sound good and some won't – let your ear be your guide.

ALTERED 9TH AND 13TH CHORDS

The previous 9th and 13th chords used extension notes that were found naturally in the scale of the chord. However, one of the primary aspects of "jazz" is to create more tension by using notes that are outside the natural notes of the scale. These are called altered notes, because they are altered either ½ step up (sharp, or #) or ½ step down (flat, or b). Common notes that get altered are the 9th, the 4th, the 5th and the 13th. Because jazz theory can get very complex very quickly, we're just going to scratch the surface with three alterations: the b9th, the #9th and the b13th.

When extensions are added to a chord, they have to be spelled out specifically, so you will see chord symbols like this:

F7b9(b13)	F A C Eb Gb Db
F7#9(b13)	F A C Eb G# Db

NOTE: So, how do you play a chord with six notes when your ukulele only has four strings? Obviously, you have to leave notes some out, and the least significant notes are usually the root (1) and the 5th. This is commonly done in jazz and they are called *rootless chords* or *rootless voicings*.

Homonyms

Due to some strange mathematical relationships that I won't go into here, the same 9th and the 13th chord forms from the previous section can be used as altered 9th and 13th chords that are 3½ steps away (or a **tritone**, if you want to investigate that). We briefly introduced chord homonyms in Chapter 5, where we saw that a Cmaj6 chord and an Am7 chord share all the same notes. The 9th and 13th chords, and their altered cousins in this section, work on the same principle, but only share a subset of notes. Here are some examples:

Ex. 64 Dominant homonyms

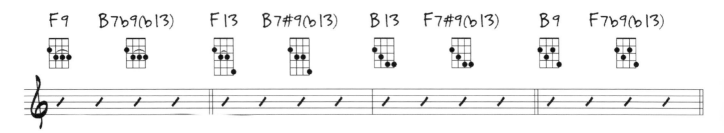

The easiest way to start hearing these altered sounds is to put them in a musical context. Let's play them in a basic I V I progression.

Ex. 65 Homonym examples in a I V I

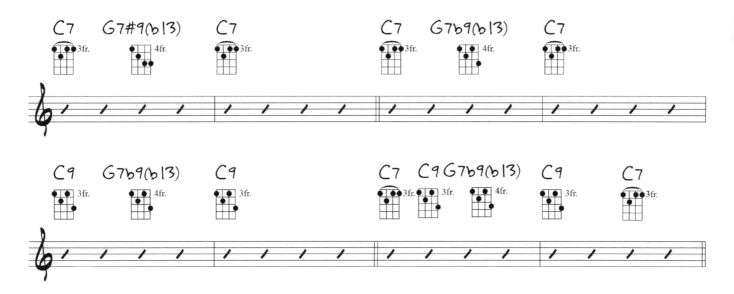

NOTE: Notice the parallel movement between the I and the V chord in the last two examples, where the same chord shape is moved one fret up or down. Another quirky side effect of the mathematical relationship mentioned above.

Here is the same exercise in the key of F, with some different chord forms.

Ex. 66 Homonym examples in F

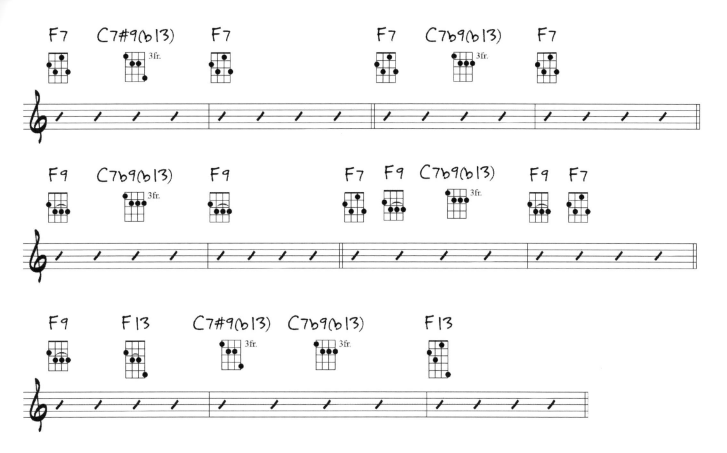

Lastly, here is a ii V I progression in G with some variations using altered chords.

Ex. 67 Homonym examples in G

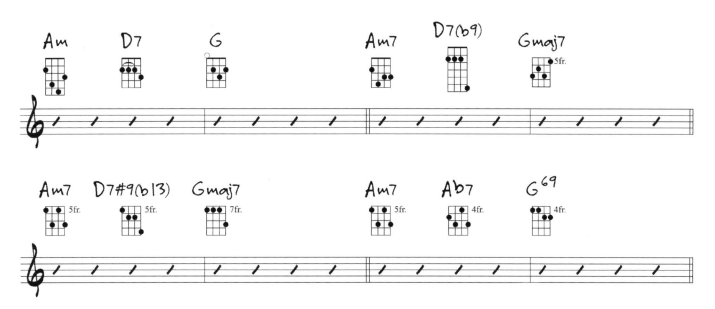

Experiment with adding these altered chords in place of dominant 7th chords in song you already know. Keep in mind that alterations and extensions are like spices when you're cooking – garlic and hot peppers are tasty in the right amounts, but they're not for everything!

THE 6/9 CHORD

Take a look at the last chord in the previous example, the 6/9 chord. It has a unique, open sound and is a very versatile chord shape. As the name implies, it has both the 6th and the 9th, but also notice that it has no 7th. The lack of the 7th in the chord adds to the soft quality.

As mentioned before, this chord shape is pretty versatile. Let's look at a few examples of how it can be used.

The same shape can be played in three different places for the same chord.

Play the following examples for an F6/9 chord.

Ex. 68 6/9 chord examples

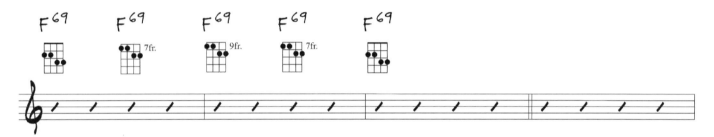

These all work as F6/9 chords. (The first two are true 6/9 chords, and even though the 3rd version contains the 7th of the chord, it still works in context as a 6/9.)

Some shapes double as two kinds of chords.

Take a look at the different positions for the C6/9 chord:

Ex. 69 6/9 chord examples

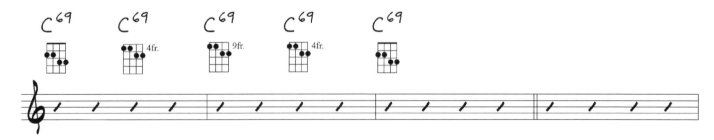

And now compare them to the F6/9 positions. The 6/9 chord shape at the 2nd fret is the same for F and C, and the shape at the 9th fret is also the same for both. How is this possible? Well, if you look at the notes available in each chord (including the 7th), you see that they overlap quite a bit.

	1	3	5	6	9	7
C 6/9	C	E	G	A	D	B
F 6/9	F	A	C	D	G	E

So, you have the common notes C D E G A in each chord. This is one reason why 6/9 chords have that open, vague quality. (Bonus tip: If you rearrange the notes C D E G A, you an also make an Amin7 chord with a suspended 4th.)

But won't they all sound the same? Yes, played by themselves they can definitely sound like they don't have a 'home key'. But if you put them in context, they sound correct. Play these examples:

Ex. 70 Same shapes, different chords

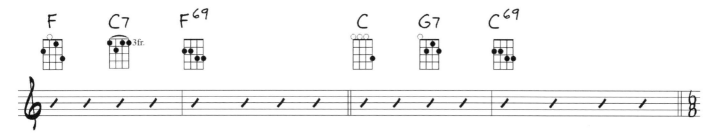

Notice how when you set up the key of F by playing an F chord and then a C7, the 6/9 chord sounds like it resolves very nicely to F. And when you set up the key of C by playing a C chord and then a G7, the same 6/9 chord resolves very nicely to C.

Harmonizing a melody line

This is a neat trick that many jazz and blues musicians use. Keep your melody on the first string and "harmonize" everything with a 6/9 chord shape. I say "harmonize" because you're not really harmonizing the melody to specific chords, you're just providing a parallel chord structure underneath the melody. And yes, it can sound very modern and different.

Try this version of "We Wish You a Merry Christmas".

Ex. 71 A modern Merry Christmas

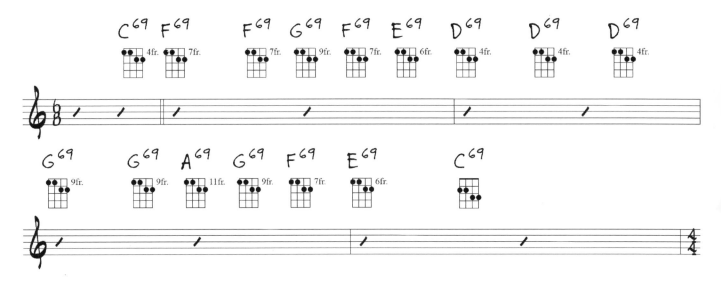

Ok, it might not be something you want to play for your grandmother, but it does create an interesting sound where the melody is the primary focus and the harmony is secondary. Some people may cringe when they hear it, but they will recognize the melody. (See if you can use this same technique to figure out the rest of the song.)

This kind of harmonizing is a little more appealing when used over minor or bluesy types of melodies, as in this last example. Notice that although it starts and ends on a C6/9, it sounds nothing like a major chord!

Ex. 72 6/9 blues riff

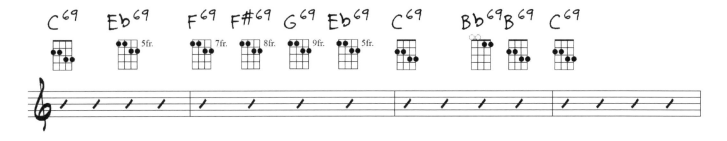

THAT'S ALL FOLKS!

Well, that wraps up Volume 2. If you've worked through all the chapters, you've added some pretty cool tricks to your ukulele playing:

- Playing chords in several locations around the neck
- Major 7th, minor 7th, and diminished 7th chords
- One and two-chord vamps, passing chords, and cycles
- Chord melodies
- Moving lines
- Suspended chords
- Extended 9th and 13th chords

These techniques can take a while to smoothly integrate into your playing – some of them will come easily and some will take a while. Just keep looking for places to substitute different voicings and positions and to add melodies and moving lines. Before you know it, they will start to pop up in your playing without even thinking about it.

Here are some ways to trigger new ideas:

- Create your own compositions
- Play a song in all keys
- Play a song in one key in three different positions
- Play a song with no 7th chords and then with all 7th chords
- Play a song and add passing chords wherever possible
- Try all the exercises with different strumming patterns
- Try all of them with fingerpicking patterns

Keep practicing and good luck!

Manufactured by Amazon.ca
Bolton, ON